MANAGING
CHANGE

THE SUNDAY TIMES
BUSINESS SKILLS SERIES

"excellent ... well worth reading"

Christopher Lorenz, the *Financial Times*

The Sunday Times Business Skills Series is an up-to-the-minute collection of books covering essential management topics in the three key areas of total quality management, personal skills and leadership skills.

Combining current management theory and practice with detailed case examples and practical advice, each book provides a definitive stand-alone summary of best management practice in a specific field. While each book is complete in itself, books in the series have been carefully co-ordinated to complement *The Sunday Times* Business Skills video training package of the same name produced by Taylor Made Films (see inside back flap for more details).

Books already published in the series:

PERFORMANCE APPRAISALS
Martin Fisher
ISBN 0 7494 1441 3

MANAGING CHANGE
Philip Sadler
ISBN 0 7494 1343 3

EFFECTIVE NEGOTIATING
Colin Robinson
ISBN 0 7494 1344 1

BUILDING YOUR TEAM
Rupert Eales-White
ISBN 0 7494 1342 5

ACHIEVING BS EN ISO 9000
Peter Jackson and David Ashton
ISBN 0 7494 1440 5

MANAGING CHANGE

Philip Sadler

KOGAN
PAGE

First published in 1995

Apart from any fair dealing for the purposes of research or private study, or criticism or review, as permitted under the Copyright, Designs and Patents Act, 1988, this publication may only be reproduced, stored or transmitted, in any form or by any means, with the prior permission in writing of the publishers, or in the case of reprographic reproduction in accordance with the terms of licences issued by the Copyright Licensing Agency. Enquiries concerning reproduction outside those terms should be sent to the publishers at the undermentioned address:

Kogan Page Limited
120 Pentonville Road
London N1 9JN

© Philip Sadler, 1995

British Library Cataloguing in Publication Data

A CIP record for this book is available from the British Library.

ISBN 0 7494 1343 3

Typeset by Saxon Graphics Ltd, Derby.
Printed in England by Clays Ltd, St Ives plc

Contents

65 → 76
99 → 119
137 → 151

Acknowledgements

I would like to acknowledge the assistance I have received from the following:

Fred Crawley, Chairman, Alliance & Leicester Building Society.

Richard Robson, Chief Executive Fermec Plc.

Colonel Richard Rook OBE of The Royal Logistic Corps.

Alan Underwood, British Telecom.

I have also received considerable help from the following people for which I thank them.

Don Beattie, Personnel Director, ICL Ltd.

David Bower, Personnel Director, Rover Group.

Andrew Mayo, Director of Human Resource Development, ICL Ltd.

Steve Rick, Assistant Director Personnel, Royal Bank of Scotland.

Roy Williams, BP.

I would also like to take this opportunity to thank Kim Bennett for her untiring efforts in preparing my last three manuscripts.

Philip Sadler
Berkhamsted
1994

Introduction

Change takes many forms and comes from many directions. A single change in the business environment can bring about a serious crisis:

- A competitor launches a new, superior product.
- Another competitor develops a much more cost-effective manufacturing process and slashes its prices.
- New competitors spring up from unexpected sources.
- A new piece of legislation poses a serious threat.
- A health-hazard is discovered which reveals that one of your key activities is seriously dangerous to health.
- Exchange rates move rapidly against you.
- And many more.

Today, any one organization probably faces several such changes simultaneously.

Rather late in the day we are learning that to survive, let alone build future prosperity, we have to become as skilled in the management of change as in the management of ongoing operations.

This book is about managing change successfully. It is designed as a companion text to the *Sunday Times* Business Skills/Taylor Made Films video of the same title. The video features four real-life case studies of change – the Alliance & Leicester Building Society, British Telecom, Fermec, and The Royal Logistic Corps. These cases are included here in Chapter 9 and are updated to mid 1994.

The 'logic' of the book is as follows.

Chapter 1 – Why Change? – looks at the reasons why change is on the agenda for so many organizations today, distinguishing between the underlying causes which reflect turbulence in the economic, technological, political and social environments, and 'triggers for change', ie the particular events which galvanize management into action.

Effective change management must be based on as deep as possible an understanding of the nature of organizations as systems and of the interactions between structure, process and culture. This is the subject matter of Chapter 2.

Chapter 3 explores the nature of organizational change, together with its relationship to corporate purpose and business strategy. The various types of change – transformational, incremental, proactive and reactive – are discussed and the impact of change on people is examined.

Given the key role of corporate culture in any attempt to achieve real change, Chapter 4 focuses on the nature of culture, its origins, and the process of changing it, with examples from the private and public sectors.

Chapter 5 discusses how a climate receptive of change can be established and looks at the early stages of the change process. The question of how to mobilize energy and commitment for change in the absence of serious crisis is addressed. The part played by visioning and mission statements is explained.

In recent years two 'holistic' approaches to change management have been widely adopted – Total Quality Management (TQM) and Business Process Re-engineering (BPR). These are discussed, with examples of their application, in Chapter 6.

Change as a way of life and the concept of the learning organization are covered in Chapter 7, while Chapter 8 deals with issues of implementation including such matters as where to start, the role of training, the part played by the human resource function and the critical importance of leadership.

Finally, Chapter 9 contains the four case studies referred to previously.

Mark Twain once said 'Most of the bad things in my life never happened.' It can also be said that most of the cases of corporate transformation never happened. Fundamental and radical change tends to be planned, discussed, publicized and started, but only rarely carried through and sustained.

Peter Block[1] surveying the US scene argues that despite the 'hype' surrounding total quality, visionary leadership and the customer-driven organization, real and lasting change in the workplace has been limited and has reached only a small proportion of the workforce.

Similarly Richard Pascale[2], writing in 1991, said 'Ford stands alone in appearing to have truly transformed itself.'

Some business leaders on both sides of the Atlantic have reputations as champions of radical change which owe more to the imagination of their public affairs departments than to their concrete achievements. Many of the anecdotal accounts of successful transformation provided by speakers at expensive one-day conferences on strategic change score highly on presentation but poorly on substance. All too many shop-floor-level workers and supervisors in so-called transformed companies have yet to become aware of the fact.

With one or two exceptions the cases and examples quoted in this book reflect initiatives taken in the late 1980s or early 1990s. It is, therefore, premature to reach a judgement as to whether the changes are truly transforming and sustainable. The most notable exceptions in the UK are British Airways, ICL and Rover. All three organizations set out to achieve radical change in the mid 1980s or earlier and have achieved remarkable turnarounds in business performance – in ways which reflect deep-seated changes in their cultures as well as other kinds of change. Their success reflects consistency in top management's commitment to change and genuine striving to bring about organizational renewal in the roundest sense – not only improving the bottom line beyond recognition, but also increasing the quality of working life for the members of the organization at all levels and giving the customer real value.

This aspect of modern business leadership sometimes receives less attention than the resolute pursuit of self interest by others whose commitment is to their own careers rather than to the organizations they are paid to serve.

Block uses the term 'stewardship' to describe the activity of business leaders who place service before self interest. This book is dedicated to those who exemplify stewardship in the UK today.

References

1. Block, P (1993) *Stewardship*, Berrett Koehler, San Francisco.

2. Pascale, Richard T (1991) *Managing on the Edge*, Penguin Books, London.

1

Why Change?

In autumn 1986 a warehouse fire at Sandoz's premises in Basle resulted in 30 tonnes of toxic chemicals leaking into the Rhine. The water turned red for miles and all life in the affected part of the river was destroyed. The public sense of outrage was enormous and revealed a pent-up hostility to the chemical industry.

Carol Kennedy[1] has described how the board of directors of another chemical concern based in Basle – Ciba-Geigy – were shaken by the strength of the reaction. It forced them to face the fact that the world around them had changed fundamentally and that attitudes to the costs as well as the benefits of industrial activity and economic growth had undergone a profound transformation.

The outcome was a board decision that Ciba-Geigy, too, must change. This decision was based on more than the perceived need to adjust company policies in response to changing social attitudes. The fire and the response to it can be seen as the 'trigger' for change but it was soon appreciated that changes in the environment, with implications for the future of the business, were many and various. It was also recognised that while these changes had been taking place the company had, relatively speaking, been standing still. The president, in stating the case for *radical* change, acknowledged that over the decades the company had grown complacent and bureaucratic.

This experience is a common one. In response to the question 'Why change?' most organizations can point to one or two particularly obvious or immediate causal factors. These are the *triggers*, the precipitating factors, but for most organizations the strongest forces for change are those stemming from immense and rapid changes to several aspects of their business environment. It is useful to look at these and their implications before considering how organizations should respond.

CHANGES IN THE ECONOMIC ENVIRONMENT

It is important to distinguish between short-term or cyclical change and longer-term structural or fundamental change. This is because although short-term changes may well call for related changes on the part of organizations, they will not normally require radical shifts in strategic direction. The longer-term changes, however, will almost certainly result in the need to revise the organization's strategic thinking and in consequence call for more fundamental changes in the organization's policies and practices.

Short-Term, Cyclical Changes

These include such volatile elements in the economic environment as:

- the business cycle;
- interest rates;
- exchange rates;
- property values;
- inflation;
- levels of taxation.

In theory, the appropriate response to such changes is tactical rather than strategic, with the implication that radical change can be avoided. In practice a very severe recession or a collapse in property values may give rise to radical cost-cutting programmes, involving plant closures and redundancies. In such cases the alternative to major change is quite simply (and quite quickly) extinction.

In the modern world periods of economic stability are rare indeed, with the result that top managements spend a great deal of time and energy 'fire-fighting' as they develop tactical responses to these short-term shifts. Unfortunately this distracts them from paying attention to the underlying trends which in the long run may prove a much more serious threat to the organization's continued existence.

Richard Pascale[2] has given us an apt analogy – the case of the boiled frog. If you put a frog in a pot of cold water and bring it very very slowly to the boil the creature will make no attempt to escape and will eventually die. This is because the change in temperature is so gradual that the frog cannot sense it. Similarly some of the really significant changes that are taking place as we approach the 21st century are so gradual that they escape the notice of decision-makers.

Longer-Term, Underlying Changes

Among the most important under this heading are:

O *Underlying growth rates*. Boom and recession tend to conceal the fact that in almost every part of the world per capita income increases from one decade to the next. This is significant in the developed world in terms of its impact on the structure of demand as the proportion of disposable income available for discretionary spending increases. It is of even greater significance in developing countries. As growth takes place in China, for example, what is potentially the world's largest market is beginning to develop very rapidly.

O *The globalization of markets*. Improvements in communications have led to the growth of transnational business with the consequence that for many industries the market for their products or services is now world-wide, while there remain few domestic industries that are not now faced by competition from overseas. At the time of writing, Britain's major food-retailing companies face the prospect of intense competition from US discount specialists. It is not difficult to predict major change on the horizon for this industry.

○ *Regional economies*. The European Community has become a major force for change. Partly this results from efforts to create 'a level playing field' in the interests of fair and free competition between member states. Partly it is a function of the new opportunities for mergers, alliances and joint ventures.

○ *New sources of competition*. In a number of industries the status quo has been radically disrupted by the growth of competition from unlikely, non-traditional sources. Nowhere is this more evident than in the field of financial services. In recent years, for example, the traditional credit-card issuing companies (banks and American Express) have been challenged by such unlikely competitors as General Motors and AT&T in the US and the *Sunday Times* in Britain. AT&T has moved from a standing start to become the major issuer of credit cards in America in just three years. In Britain, Marks & Spencer is now a major source of personal finance and pension plans.

○ *Deindustrialization*. Since the 1960s (even earlier in the US) an important long-term trend in the developed economies has been the relative decline in manufacturing and the relative growth in the service sector. This in turn reflects a number of other underlying trends:

— the industrialization of the Third World means that more and more manufacturing is taking place in countries like Malaysia, South Korea, Brazil, Taiwan and Indonesia.

— as people's standards of living rise they tend to spend disproportionately more of their incomes on services such as banking, insurance, travel, and leisure pursuits. At the same time industry itself makes growing use of such services as advertising, design, consultancy and facilities management.

If we pause and consider the implications of these longer-term trends for one UK company – Rolls Royce Plc – we can see how sooner or later they will necessitate strategic change.

Long-term economic growth will determine the rate of growth in the world demand for air travel, and differential growth rates will determine which nations will be the major purchasers of aircraft engines. Who, in the 1960s, would have predicted Singapore and Hong Kong as major world-players in the airline industry? China's future development is an obvious market to go for in the longer term but there will be some surprise entrants also.

The industry is already a global one with three major players – GE, Pratt and Whitney, and Rolls Royce. Already joint ventures and strategic alliances are being formed. The future will see growing involvement in the industry on the part of Japanese and German companies. Mergers are not beyond possibility.

Given cost pressures and political influences another issue facing the company is the question of where to locate any expansion of its manufacturing activities. Would having plants in Japan or the US increase the company's chances of having its products chosen by national airlines in those countries? Are there countries where the level of skill in the workforce would meet Rolls Royce's exacting quality requirements but with a significantly lower labour cost than in the UK?

On one hand, none of the above issues has necessarily to be resolved within a short time-scale. On the other hand if the company ignored them its own long-term future might be in danger.

TECHNOLOGICAL CHANGES

A company like Rolls Royce does not only face the prospect of having to change because of economic reasons. There are other forces at work, not the least of which is technological progress.

Technological change is of three basic kinds:

1. *New processes for manufacturing goods or delivering services.* Under this heading come not only new forms of 'hardware' such as automation equipment in the factory or automatic cash dispensers in retail banking, but also new technologies

such as the 'just-in-time' method of inventory control which are more to do with systems and procedures than with machinery.

2. *New products and significantly improved products resulting from advances in technology and/or science.* In recent years the list includes compact discs, mobile phones, a whole range of new ethical drugs and low-cost personal computers.

3. *Developments in the technology for processing and transmitting information.* This includes information technology (IT) which combines computers and telecommunications. These developments are to do with both hardware and software and have consequences for all organizations, large or small.

POLITICAL CHANGES

These are occurring at every level – global, regional, national and at the level of local communities.

Some of the things that have affected many British businesses and public sector organizations in the past decade or so include:

○ privatization;

○ deregulation;

○ the reduction of East–West political tensions and military preparedness following the collapse of communist regimes;

○ the Gulf War;

○ the conflict in the former Yugoslavia;

○ diplomatic problems with foreign governments (eg Malaysia);

○ various political (as distinct from military or economic) decisions to purchase or not to purchase military aircraft manufactured in the UK.

The Royal Logistic Corps case (Chapter 9) offers a good example of the impact of political decisions in bringing about major change in a traditional setting.

Change in the Civil Service

Currently the Government's programme for the reform of the Civil Service involves questioning almost every aspect of a civil servant's working life. Large-scale changes are under way in the context of the shifting of a great deal of activity from the public to the private sector.

There are three main strands to the Government's programme:

1. Pushing responsibility and accountability for performance closer to the point of service delivery. This involves the creation of 'Next Steps' executive agencies with enhanced managerial discretion within defined performance standards.

2. Getting close to customer needs and expectations. This includes the Citizen's Charter, calling for a greater openness and a focus on improving service quality.

3. The 'Competing for Quality' initiative which seeks to test services against market criteria and, in appropriate cases, contracting out non-core activities.

As a consequence the traditional Civil Service way of centrally-ordained and uniformly applied policies and practices is being challenged and dismantled. The customary obedience to rules is being replaced by the requirement for flexibility and innovation. Hierarchical structures are being flattened and teamworking is replacing functional departments. New performance standards are being developed.

SOCIAL CHANGES

Last, but by no means least in importance, are social changes.

These take various forms. One aspect of social change consists of changes in people's *attitudes, values* and *beliefs*. Long-term changes in Western countries over the past two or three decades include:

○ Much greater emphasis on health and safety – with the result that huge changes have been forced on such industries as tobacco, food manufacturing and retailing, motor vehicle manufacturing, construction and civil engineering.

○ A steadily growing concern for the environment. Here the major industries which have had to adjust include the oil industry, the chemical industry, electricity generation, motor vehicle manufacturing and fishing.

○ A growing demand, backed by legislation, on the part of women and members of ethnic minorities, for equality of treatment and equality of opportunity.

A second aspect of social change is in the field of *social institutions*. In most societies the most fundamental social institution is the family and it is at the level of family life that some of the most profound social changes have been taking place. The increase in the divorce rate, the decline of parental authority, the growth in the number of single parent families and the separation of older people from their families have created enormous challenges for the public sector, particularly education and social services.

There have also been profound changes to the third aspect of social change, the *social structure* – particularly the age structure. The full implications of our ageing society have yet to be grasped, particularly in terms of its impact on the National Health Service.

The fourth area of social change is that of *patterns of behaviour*. Demand for goods and services is very much a function of people's lifestyles. It is generally predicted that people will spend more and more on leisure activities as living standards rise, that second holidays will become much more common, and that more and more people will become involved in keeping fit. Unfortunately it is also confidently predicted that crime rates – particularly crimes involving violence – will continue to grow and that the already huge cost to industry of theft, fraud and sheer vandalism is likely to increase in the years ahead.

TURBULENT ENVIRONMENTS

The word 'turbulent' has come to describe an environment characterized both by several changes occurring rapidly and simultaneously and by a situation such that only the most optimistic see the possibility of a return to a more stable environment in the foreseeable future. Figure 1.1 shows such a turbulent environment in the case of IBM.

The impact of all this change on the once invulnerable giant corporation is now well known – financial losses on a massive scale, downsizing and loss of its position as one of America's most admired companies in the annual *Fortune* survey. IBM is now fighting back and facing the need for continuous and fundamental change if it is to recover its previous pre-eminence in its field.

Past	Present
Few customers	Millions of customers
Traditional competition	Thousands of competitors
Predictable technological change	Exploding rate of change
Hardware - dominated	Software / Systems / Solutions
Direct sales force	Business partners / alliances
One set of terms and conditions	Many ways of doing business

Figure 1.1 IBM: An example of rapid and radical change in the business environment

TRIGGERS FOR CHANGE

Edgar Wille[3] of the Ashridge Management Research Group identified the principal triggers for change in 178 organizations, of which 93 were British, 31 were from continental Europe and 54 from North America. They included public sector organizations and private companies from a wide range of industries. The results are shown in Table 1.1.

Table 1.1 Triggers for change

	UK	Other Europe	N. America	Total
	n=93	n=31	n=54	n=178
	%	%	%	%
Financial loss/ drop in profits	22	27	26	24
Increased competition/ loss of market share	15	32	31	23
Industry in recession	10	3	–	6
New chief executive officer	15	16	18	16
Proactive (opportunities or events foreseen)	15	26	30	23
Technological development	11	1	3	8
Staff utilization	10	–	–	5

EXAMPLES FROM THE ASHRIDGE CASES

Trigger	*Companies*
Financial losses	British Airways, ICI, ICL, Jaguar, Olivetti, Chrysler, Wickes
Increased competition	Rank Xerox, JCB, Motorola, Swatch, Fagor (Spain), Polaroid, Jacobs-Suchard, Schneider (France), AT&T, General Motors, IBM
Recession	Massey Ferguson
New chief executive officer	BP, ICI, London Life, ASEA, Haltel, SAS, General Electric, United Technologies
Proactive	Prudential Corporation, Thistle Hotels, TSB, Digital
Technological development	Courage, Duracell, Fiat

Some Further Examples

In British local government, Brent Council's trigger for change was a financial crisis in 1988 resulting in 1000 job losses out of a total payroll of 7000, leaving basic services in disarray[4].

In the early 1980s ICL, the UK's major computer manufacturer, very nearly went out of business. The company was making losses, it was running out of cash and had no products that customers wanted to buy[5].

Milliken in the US won the prestigious Baldrige Award for quality in 1989. The trigger for change in this case was a visit to Japan in 1981 by chairman George Milliken. He was shaken by the evidence he found of superior quality on the part of the

23

Japanese and on his return to America engaged quality specialist Philip Crosby to advise the company[6].

In the case of Rover Group[7] the triggers for change were:

○ poor financial performance such that long-term survival was becoming increasingly doubtful;

○ a deserved reputation for poor quality;

○ chronic serious industrial relations problems;

○ intensifying competition, particularly from Japan;

○ moving from public ownership to the private sector;

○ the appointment of a new chairman and a new managing director.

In the case of the Xerox Corporation[8] the trigger was a profits collapse in the face of Japanese competition – from $1.149bn in 1980 to $600m in 1981.

In 1983 in another UK local government case at Braintree[9] the closure of one large firm with the loss of 4000 jobs was a huge blow to the local economy. The Council did not have the financial resources to respond with immediate solutions but did recognize the need to create the conditions for a more prosperous future. A process was started with the title Braintree Means Business.

In the case of a major UK Brewery, Ind-Coope in Burton[10], the trigger was changes in the market-place, with customers requiring more products in more packages in more countries at lower cost and with a more rapid response.

In the case of optical instrument manufacturers Barr and Stroud[11] their old inefficient factory was the only industrial site in a middle-class suburban area. In 1990, they sold it to Safeway and placed a contract for a new factory on a green-field site. The move to the new factory created a wonderful opportunity to bring about some radical changes.

In 1980 Ford incurred a $2.2bn loss, the largest in US corporate history[12]. At one point its cash reserves were down so low the company would have remained solvent for only 45 days. 'You can never underestimate how scared we were in 1980 and 1981. We really believed Ford could die.'

References

1. Kennedy, Carol 'Changing the company culture at Ciba-Geigy', *Long Range Planning* Vol 26 No 1 February 1990.

2. Pascale, Richard T (1991) *Managing on the Edge,* Penguin Books, London.

3. Wille, Edgar (1989) *Triggers for Change,* Ashridge Management Research Group, Berkhamsted.

4. van de Vliet, Anita, 'The Brent Conversion', *Management Today,* March 1994.

5. Beattie, DF and Tampoe, FMK 'Human resource planning for ICL', *Long Range Planning* Vol 23 No 1 February 1990.

6. Caulkin, Simon, 'The road to peerless Wigan', *Management Today,* March 1994.

7. Bower, David 'Becoming a learning organization – the experience of the Rover Group' in Philip Sadler (ed) (1993) *Learning More About Learning Organizations,* AMED, London.

8. Walker, Rob 'Rank Xerox – management revolution', *Long Range Planning* Vol 25 No 1 February 1992.

9. Bailey, Michael (1994) *Total Management – Putting People First,* paper presented at AMED Annual Conference, Warwick.

10. Cox, David L 'Doubling productivity at a major brewery', *Long Range Planning* Vol 23 No 4 August 1990.

11. Pickard, Jane 'From strife to smooth sailing', *Personnel Management* December 1993.

12. Pascale, Richard T *op. cit.*

2

Understanding Organizations

INTRODUCTION

We live in a world where we take organizations for granted. As children our first experience of an organization is probably with a school. For some it is a hospital. In early life we become customers of organizations when we buy sweets at Woolworths or pass through the turnstiles to watch our favourite soccer team. Later on we may move from school to university and experience life as a member of a much larger and far more complex organization. When we start work, most of us do so in the employment of an organization – in industry, in the public sector, in the armed services, in the Church or perhaps in the voluntary or charity sector. As adults we have many kinds of encounters with organizations – central and local government agencies, the police, the health service, banks, building societies, the utilities, retailers, construction firms, the postal service – the list is endless. We take them for granted. We do not usually stop to think why organizations exist or what exactly an organization *is*, anyway.

Do we need a better understanding of the nature of organizations and their impact on our lives? The answer for most of us is probably 'Yes'. It is certainly 'Yes', however, if we become involved in the management of an organization and even more so if we are concerned with managing organizational change.

THE ORIGINS OF ORGANIZATION

For thousands of years people have coped with tasks which have involved co-ordinating the activities of large numbers of individuals. In response to this challenge we have designed complex social institutions called organizations. Until relatively recently these existed mainly in three spheres – the affairs of state, the armed forces and the Church. With the industrial revolution, however, came a new type of complex task – the need to co-ordinate the activities of hundreds or even thousands of workers in the process of wealth creation.

At the heart of organization design are two basic approaches to dealing with the complexity of the task. The first is breaking down the decision-making process by means of the *delegation of authority*. In Exodus in the Old Testament, Moses' father-in-law Jethro watched him sitting in judgement day after day while the people queued to present their petitions and seek judgement. He told Moses that it was impossible for him to cope with all the decision-making by himself and advised him to appoint able men to be rulers of thousands, rulers of hundreds, and rulers of tens. Since that time almost all organizations of any size have been characterized by a hierarchical system of authority and control.

The second basic approach is to break down the work of the organization into tasks capable of being carried out efficiently by individuals and work groups – the process of the *division of labour*. Adam Smith in *The Wealth of Nations* used the example of the trade of pin-maker. He pointed out that, working alone, a skilled worker could make but one pin a day. Once the task was broken down into its various operations such as drawing wire, cutting it, grinding the point – 18 operations in all – then a team of ten, with these various tasks allocated among them, could make some 48,000 pins a day.

Since Adam Smith's time industrial and commercial organizations have developed considerably. They have grown in size – British Telecom employs over 150,000 people in the UK. In the public sector Britain's largest employer is the National Health Service with approximately 1,000,000 employees.

Many organizations have operations in many different countries. They often have very wide product ranges. They may serve several different markets simultaneously, selling their goods or services to governments, to industry or direct to consumers. They co-ordinate a far wider range of skills than in Adam Smith's pin factory. As well as the various trades and skills of workers in production and maintenance there are salespeople, research workers, accountants, engineers, lawyers, personnel managers, and specialists in logistics, security, health and safety, property and public relations.

The development of effective organizations to handle this complexity has been a major factor in improving living standards in the First World. Important as particular advances in science and technology are, it is the harnessing of technology through organization which has transformed human productivity and raised living standards. No new discovery can be exploited nor any new product developed without organization. The problems involved in organization design are every bit as complex as those involved in writing software, designing machinery or developing new drugs. There is no recipe, however, or set of rules for the design of effective organizations any more than there is a set of rules for writing symphonies.

CHARACTERISTIC FEATURES OF ORGANIZATIONS

As well as the hierarchical structure of decision-making and the division of labour, organizations have other characteristic features, as follows.

1. *Organizations are social institutions*. They consist of groups of people whose activities are directed towards the achievement of a common purpose. Those who design organizations often tend to concern themselves only with those aspects of the human being which relate to his or her ability to perform an allotted task and thus contribute to the work of the organization as a whole. This might include aptitudes, skills and a range of personal attributes such as honesty, reliability and diligence. Human beings, however, bring their whole selves to work. Their relationships of friendship or hostility with

co-workers, their family obligations and concerns, their fears and hopes for the future are all part of organizational life.

The structure which has been designed to facilitate decision-making and the efficient execution of tasks will have other functions for those who work within it – it will act as a career structure for the ambitious and as a status system. To change the structure will not only change working arrangements, it will also change people's career prospects and their status.

The organization will often have central importance in the lives of many of its members, especially those who spend the greater part of their working lives within a single organization. In consequence they may come to see it as existing for their benefit – to provide them with security, income, advancement and status – rather than to serve the public or provide a good return on investors' funds. Where such attitudes have developed the process of managing organizational change is likely to prove particularly difficult and resistance to change particularly strong.

As a member of an organization a person does more than simply fill a job. He or she is also the incumbent of a role. An organizational role can be defined as 'a set of expectations held by others concerning the behaviour of the incumbent of a particular role in a social system.'

The expectations that an organization has of an employee will nearly always cover aspects of behaviour in addition to those purely concerned with carrying out a particular task. This, the *formal* role, may include such other matters as the rights and obligations associated with the job (for example period of notice, whether monthly paid or hourly paid, eligibility for overtime payments), dress and deportment (for example the requirement for men to wear dark suits and sober ties and for women not to wear trousers) and status (for example whether or not a person is allocated a reserved parking space).

This last aspect of the role is particularly important in relation to people's emotional responses to change. Almost without exception organizations have formal status systems which exercise a strong influence on behaviour. This system is supported by powerful practices and symbols, such as different places to eat, the allocation of company cars and the entitlement to secretarial assistance.

Other aspects of organizational roles are *informal* – they have grown up over time and have become accepted and established without any conscious decision-processes having been involved. An example in many traditional organizations, which has only recently started to be challenged, is that it is part of a secretary's role to make the tea and coffee.

It is often the case that quite important aspects of a person's role are not written down. Often they are simply part of the culture. New employees learn about them during induction processes or subsequently (sometimes painfully) from their co-workers.

When introducing change it is vitally important to be sensitive to the informal as well as the formal aspects of roles.

2. *Organizations are 'socio-technical' systems.* In practice, work in organizations is carried out by a partnership between human beings and technology. By 'technology' I mean both hardware and software – the processes of production and administration which involve a combination of equipment and machinery on the one hand and a wide range of systems and procedures on the other. Production technology, for example, involves both the machinery involved and systems for production control and the maintenance of equipment.

    Technology both influences and is influenced by the process of organization design. To change the technology inevitably results in changes to the social system, while in order to achieve desired changes to the social system it will usually be necessary to make changes in the technology used or at least in the way it is used.

3. *Organizations endure.* They have an existence independent from the people who are their members at any given point in time.

Organizations may not survive indefinitely but they do usually survive longer than the working lives of individual members. Marks & Spencer today is clearly recognizable as the same organization that existed under that name in the 1960s, yet most of its current employees were not members of the organization at that time. The company has expanded, changed in many respects, moved into new spheres of activity such as food retailing and financial services, yet is still recognizably Marks & Spencer.

This existence independently of the people who are members is evident in another way. When one employee leaves he or she is almost always immediately replaced by another without necessitating any change to the way the organization works. This is because in a very real sense the organization consists of a set of roles rather than of a number of human beings each with his or her idiosyncratic characteristics.

THE COMPONENTS OF ORGANIZATION

When organizational change takes place it will involve changes in any or all of the following:

○ structure;

○ systems and procedures;

○ culture.

Figure 2.1 illustrates the interdependence of these three aspects of organization and how they relate to strategy. BP uses the analogy of a three-legged stool – take one leg away and the whole thing collapses.

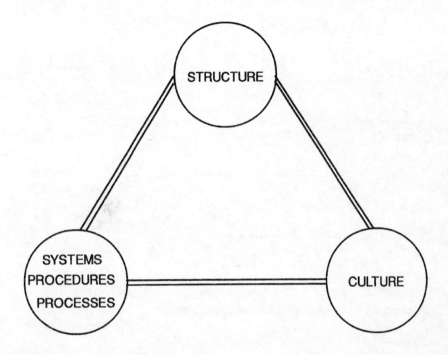

Figure 2.1   The components of organization

THE ELEMENTS OF STRUCTURE

Hierarchy

The traditional model of organization is illustrated in Figure 2.2.

The levels or layers which are involved in an organization's hierarchical structure exist, at least in theory, to define levels of authority and associated responsibility. Professor Eliott Jaques[1] has made a special study of the decision-making process in organizations based on his theory of 'the time-span of discretion'. This theory asserts that there exist clearly distinct levels of authority in organizations which are related to the length of time which elapses between a decision being taken and its outcome becoming known. At the shop-floor-level a worker's decision when operating a machine or using a tool will be shown to be correct or otherwise almost immediately. At the other end of the

33

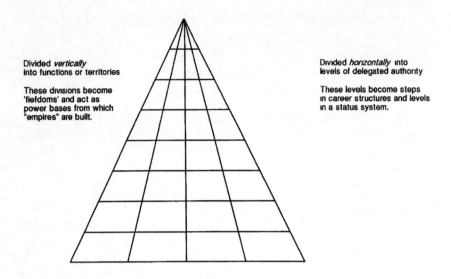

Divided *vertically* into functions or territories

These divisions become 'fiefdoms' and act as power bases from which "empires" are built.

Divided *horizontally* into levels of delegated authority

These levels become steps in career structures and levels in a status system.

Figure 2.2   The traditional model of organization

scale, decisions about investment or organization taken by the chief executive of a company like BP might take 20 years or more to work through to a result. Jaques argues that for a global enterprise on the scale of BP there are seven such levels. Many organizations have much steeper hierarchies than this. The British Army has 18 and by contrast, according to Tom Peters[2], the Swiss-based multinational engineering group ABB has only four levels in an organization employing 215,000 people. There is an executive committee at the top, including chief executive Percy Barnevick. Next come 65 business area managers, responsible for some 5000 autonomous profit centres, each of which is made up of 10-person, multifunction, high performance teams.

The layers, as well as defining levels of authority and responsibility, serve two other functions which are important to take account of when managing change.

First, these layers form steps in a career structure. A steep hierarchy offers a ladder with many rungs – an incentive for the ambitious and the prospect of frequent experience of the sense of reward and recognition that promotion brings. Organizations which reduce the number of layers, for whatever reason, restrict promotion opportunities. They encounter the paradox of 'high fliers' hitting 'low ceilings'. It becomes vital to look to other kinds of reward and recognition as substitutes.

Secondly, the layers serve as the basis for a status system. Status differences have characterized UK industry since its origins. In some organizations the degree of refinement and elaboration of the status system is quite astonishing – to the extent that one is led to believe that more management time and effort has been put into its design than into the design of some core business processes. Changing the structure – and de-layering in particular – inevitably challenges the existing 'pecking order' and this is undoubtedly a major, if unacknowledged, factor in much resistance to change.

Divisionalization: the Horizontal Dimension

The traditional model of organization (shown in Figure 2.3) also involves a structure divided by vertical boundaries. These can take a number of forms:

1. *Functional boundaries*. Historically the most common basis for internal differentiation has been the division of labour resulting in a structure based on differentiation by function. In practice this can mean one of two things:

   a) Divisions based on common skills or qualifications, for example a healthcare organization differentiated into divisions or departments of doctors, nursing staff and administration staff.

   b) Divisions based on a shared process, but with various skills or disciplines involved in a single process. This is common in manufacturing industry. A manufacturing division may include engineers, chemists and computer specialists as well as production and maintenance workers. A marketing division may employ a range of disciplines from economists to sales staff, and an administrative division may include accountants, personnel specialists and lawyers.

Functional boundaries are common in organizations in their early stages of development but tend to come under strain when the organization grows in size and/or complexity, by extending its product range, for example, or establishing overseas subsidiaries.

The main advantage of a functional structure is, of course, the concentration of expertise. Its principal disadvantage is the problem of securing the necessary level of co-operation across functional boundaries. A high level of such collaboration is essential for effective innovation and in consequence it is characteristic of functional organizations that they are slow to innovate.

Moving from divisions based on function to divisions based on some other criteria is a very common starting point for organizational change. Resistance can be expected from functional specialists who see their 'empires' being broken up.

Pascale[3] describes the intense conflict between functions that existing at Ford in the 1970s. Each division of the company was concerned chiefly with its own performance and didn't care about optimizing overall results. Disputes between Design and Car Body Engineering were legendary. Though their buildings were adjacent, officials of the two departments communicated by memo, refusing to meet face to face.

Pascale gives as an example of internal conflict Ford's attempt to make the Escort a world car in 1980 – a vehicle with common parts which could be assembled in different locations for a variety of local markets. In practice each geographical region re-designed the car. In the US only six of the Escort's 5000 parts remained in common with the European model – and one of these was the radiator cap.

It was never a question of 'Are we winning against the Japanese?' It was 'Are we winning against each other?'

2. *Other forms of internal differentiation*. The two other most common forms of divisionalization are by product/market or by territory.

Product or market divisionalization, as the term implies, involves grouping together people with a mixture of qualifications or skills and who perform various functions into divisions which focus on particular products or particular markets, or where products and markets are much the same thing.

Examples of product divisionalization include in retailing the differentiation of food retailing from DIY retailing (Sainsbury's), of cars from trucks (Volvo) and insurance from banking (National Westminster).

Common examples of divisions based on markets include differentiating prescription drugs from 'over the counter' products and differentiating children's hospitals from others such as geriatric-care institutions. Instances where products and markets are virtually the same include British Aerospace (civil and military aircraft divisions).

Divisionalization based on territory occurs at its simplest within a country when activities are grouped by geographical region. As firms move abroad a first step may be to separate an international division from a domestic division and subsequently to move to divisions based on regions of the world.

The advantages and disadvantages of the various forms of divisionalization have been studied by Bartlett and Ghoshal[4] with particular reference to international operations. They argue that the failures and disappointments of many companies in international operations is more often due to organization problems than to errors in strategy.

Functional divisionalization favours global integration of markets and manufacturing efficiency. Classic examples of unified markets which require global efficiency include transistors, radios, TVs, VCRs and quartz technology watches.

Product divisionalization favours the process of exploiting parent company know-how through world-wide diffusion of innovation along the channels created by product divisions.

Regional divisionalization favours the process of responsiveness and sensitivity to local market differences.

The Matrix Structure

Matrix organization represents an attempt to get the best of both worlds – a high level of functional expertise combined with a strong focus on a particular product, project or market segment coupled with a high level of collaboration between different divisions. A prototype matrix structure is shown in Figure 2.3.

Critics of the matrix approach argue that these supposed advantages are outweighed by the lack of clear accountability and confused loyalties involved.

Some of the problems involved with the operation of a matrix structure are:

O *Instability*. This reflects an ongoing tug-of-war between the small interdisciplinary teams and the centres of functional expertise which results in the structure being first pulled in one direction and then the other.

O *Delayed response*. When conflicts arise between product or project managers and functional chiefs they tend to be resolved by pushing decisions further up the structure. This can slow down the decision-making process.

O *Ambiguity and uncertainty*. Individuals find it difficult to cope with the ambiguity of their roles, divided loyalties and uncertainty about the locus of authority.

Frequent starting-points for organization change are either the move from a functional structure to a matrix or back from a matrix structure to some other form of organization.

Structural Devices

Other structural arrangements commonly found in organizations include the following:

1. *Project groups or task forces*. These are normally interdisciplinary groups brought into being in order to carry out a specified task, on the completion of which the group is disbanded. In some situations – particularly common in the civil engineering and construction industries – virtually all work is

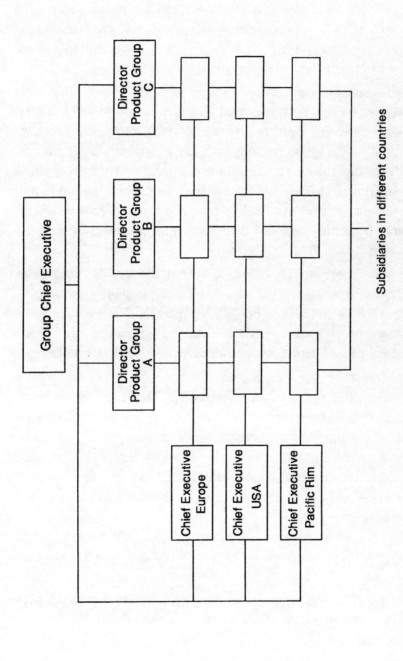

Figure 2.3   Matrix organization

carried out in this way and staff move from one project to another without having a permanent 'home' in the organization. In other cases individuals combine membership of a project team (for example, one focusing on the launch of a new product) with a more routine task and a role in a more or less permanent organizational grouping.

2. *Autonomous work groups*. These are shop-floor-level groups which, having been allocated a task, are empowered to take a wide range of decisions about working practices. They are usually held accountable for quality as well as for output and disciplinary matters. They do not normally have an appointed supervisor, although they may have an experienced and well-qualified person attached to the group who acts as a facilitator. In some instances they elect a leader from within the group.

3. *Quality circles*. This is a structural device imported from Japan. A quality circle consists of a group of employees – usually between four and 12 in number – who voluntarily meet on a regular basis to identify, investigate and solve work-related problems, particularly those to do with quality.

4. *Committees*. In contrast to project groups or task forces, committees tend to have a longer life. They focus on issues of concern to more than one department or division of an organization but which, unlike projects, tend to be a permanent feature of organizational life. Obvious examples of such issues include health and safety, security, and management succession. Committees tend to proliferate and outlast their usefulness.

When Bob Horton initiated the large scale programme of organizational change in BP in 1990 there were 86 standing committees in head office. These were reduced to six.

5. *Networks*. Networks change how and by whom key business decisions are taken. They integrate decision-making horizontally.

A network identifies the small company within the big company and empowers it to make the four-dimensional trade-offs – between functions, business units, geography, and global customers.

Normally a network will be made up of a group of managers and professionals who, by virtue of their competence, energy, drive, control of key resources and location at the critical junction points of information flows, are most qualified to deliver the corporate strategy and are totally committed to doing so.

Networks are designed to help managers evaluate problems and reach decisions from the perspective of what is right for the customer and the company rather than from narrower functional, divisional or local national interests.

SYSTEMS, PROCEDURES AND PROCESSES

These are the relatively formal, prescribed and standardized ways of doing things that have been developed or adopted by the organization. There will exist systems and procedures governing the core business processes, however these are defined. For a typical manufacturing company, for example, the key processes might be:

O business planning;

O new product development;

O product improvement;

O manufacturing;

O inbound logistics;

O outbound logistics;

O maintenance

O sales;

O after sales service;

O financial control;

O human resource management.

Under any one of these headings will exist a whole range of systems and procedures. For example the manufacturing process will involve systems and/or procedures for:

O production scheduling and control;

O quality control;

O inventory control.

The process of human resource management will involve such systems and/or procedures as:

O remuneration systems;

O performance review and appraisal systems;

O job grading systems;

O procedures for recruiting and for terminating employment.

Organizational change involves both the modification of existing systems and procedures and the introduction of new ones. In recent years, for example, large numbers of organizations have introduced a system of checks on quality – usually BS 5750 – as part of a wider programme of change aimed at improving competitiveness.

CULTURE

Culture is notoriously difficult to define. The culture of an organization is an amalgam of shared values, a common 'mindset', characteristic behaviours ('the way we do things around here') and symbols of various kinds.

Values

Values are the things that the members of an organization collectively see as important and which consequently tend to guide their behaviour.

EXAMPLES OF VALUES

product quality	order	stability
customer service	conformity	loyalty
beating the competition	change	openness
taking risks	status	profits
behaving ethically	growth	toughness
employee welfare	job security	trust
reputation	respect for authority	
flexibility	respecting the rules	

Chris Argyris[5] has pointed out that there is an important difference between values which are 'espoused' (paid lip-service to) and the deeply seated values which actually do get put into practice. It is common, in the course of organization change programmes, to draw up fine-sounding lists of values. The process of embedding such values into the culture so that they actually determine behaviour is, however, much more difficult to achieve.

Mindset, or Paradigm

This consists of a shared set of assumptions or beliefs.

For example, in the 1960s the mindset of top management in the UK car industry included the following assumptions:

O British people could be relied on to buy British cars.

O Japanese competition need not be taken seriously since Japanese products were notoriously of poor quality.

O Built-in obsolescence (such as cars that rusted badly within five years) was a sensible strategy since it encouraged people to change their cars.

O The workforce was led by communists or radical socialists. The only sensible employee relations policy was one of confrontation.

Before the UK industry could begin to compete effectively with the Japanese and with the resurgent manufacturers of France,

Italy and Germany this mindset had to change. Its resilience and deep-seated nature was perhaps the single greatest obstacle to the survival of the industry.

Characteristic Behaviours

These cover an extremely wide range. Some of the key aspects include:

O *Management style*. Is the decision making autocratic or consultative? Does management practise 'management by walking about'? Are managers' doors open or closed?

O *Dress*. Are people expected to wear formal business clothing? Is there a company uniform, Japanese-style, which masks differences in rank or status?

O *Relationships*. Do people address each other formally or informally? Do they interact socially as well as at work? How much interaction takes place across different levels in the organization?

Symbols

Among the many things which can act as symbols of a corporate culture are:

O the *image* created by corporate identity programmes, for example BP's use of green to symbolize its concern for the environment.

O the *impression* created by the corporate office, for example does it dominate the city skyline like the NatWest Tower or Shell Centre, or is it small, discreet, suburban?

Culture change is a vital element in any programme of radical or transformational organizational change. It is sufficiently complex to warrant a chapter devoted to it, therefore the nature of culture is developed further in Chapter 4.

References

1. Jaques, Eliott (1989) *Requisite Organization,* Cason Hall, Cleveland.

2. Peters, Tom (1992) *Liberation Management,* MacMillan, London.

3. Pascale, Richard T (1991) *Managing on the Edge,* Penguin Books, London.

4. Bartlett, C and Ghoshal, S (1989) *Managing Across Borders,* Hutchinson Business Books, London.

5. Argyris, Chris (1993) *On Organizational Learning,* Blackwell Business, Cambridge.

3

The Nature of Organizational Change

When dealing with the issues involved in the management of complex organizations a major source of difficulty is the lack of a common language and a set of widely accepted definitions of the key concepts. It is important, therefore, when developing a set of ideas to define the terms being used. Some basic definitions are set out here.

PURPOSE

An organization's purpose is what provides its *raison d'être*. Sometimes other words are used in this sense, for example objectives, goals, aims, and mission.

Andrew Campbell and his co-researchers[1] at the Ashridge Strategic Management Centre have pointed out that in the private sector most companies fall into one of the following groups:

1. Those which define their purpose narrowly as *serving the interests of the shareholders*. Hanson Trust is a good example. Such companies usually set themselves objectives couched in financial terms such as return on shareholders' funds or growth in earnings per share.

2. Those which define purpose more broadly as *serving the interests of the 'stakeholders'*, that is the employees, customers, suppliers and the community as well as the shareholders. Sainsbury's is a case in point.

In Britain, an inquiry entitled *Tomorrow's Company: The Role of Business in a Changing World*[2], carried out by the Royal Society of Arts, resulted in an interim report in 1994 which stated 'the conclusion reached is that to achieve success tomorrow's company must take an inclusive approach with customers, suppliers, employees, investors and the community'. It went on to assert that under the inclusive approach success cannot be defined solely in terms of the bottom line, nor can purpose be set out in relation to the interests of a single stakeholder. Among the companies sponsoring the inquiry, and thus lending their support to this approach, were not only such industrial majors as Whitbread Plc, Cadbury Ltd and British Gas but also leading financial institutions such as National Westminster Bank Plc and Kleinwort Benson Investment Management Ltd.

A recent large-scale research study carried out in the US by Kotter and Heskett at Harvard[3] and which involved tracking the performance of more than 200 companies over an 11-year period, showed that companies which had adopted the inclusive or stakeholder approach were very much more successful on several criteria than firms which stated their mission purely in terms of shareholders' interests. Over the 11-year period, organizations which emphasized obligations to stakeholders increased turnover by 682 per cent compared with an increase of 166 per cent among the rest. Their share prices rose on average by 901 per cent compared with 74 per cent and profits by 756 per cent compared with a mere 1 per cent.

3. Those which define purpose *as a philosophy* ('To be the best'), either in ethical terms such as Body Shop, or in terms of winning, such as Komatsu's well-known purpose 'to surround Caterpillar'. Such statements of purpose have in common their function in motivating employees and building commitment to the achievement of something worthwhile.

In the public sector things are more complicated. The taxpayer stands in some senses in the role of shareholder, but with some possible exceptions public sector organizations do not see the needs of the taxpayer as the reason for their existence. Formally the purposes of public bodies are stated in Acts of Parliament or regulations of various kinds. Less formally it may seem obvious that hospitals exist to provide healthcare and schools to provide education. In practice, life is much more complex and very careful consideration needs to be given to statements of purpose in such organizations.

STRATEGY

A strategy (or a set of strategies) is *the means chosen for the achievement of purpose*.

Strategic management is the process of more or less consistently managing the organization over relatively long periods of time in such a way that it fulfils its purpose. At times, for example during a severe economic downturn, the sheer need to survive a crisis may mean that actions are taken which are inconsistent with the strategy. Once the crisis is past, however, the underlying strategy will be reactivated.

In cases where the purpose of a business is defined narrowly as serving shareholders' interests the focus will be mainly on 'business strategies' which will provide a means of pursuing that objective.

At corporate level the range of possible business strategies includes:

O designing the portfolio – making acquisitions and divestments so as to achieve horizontal or vertical integration or diversification;

O building the corporate image and reputation;

O balancing the claims of the stakeholders;

O alternative approaches to adding value to subsidiaries ('parenting' strategies).

At the level of the operating subsidiary or business unit the options focus on the achievements of competitive advantage and include:

O becoming the lowest cost producer in a particular market;

O differentiation via quality of product or service;

O differentiation via innovation;

O focus on a particular niche market.

These 'business strategies' will normally be supported by functional strategies such as manufacturing strategy, human resource strategy and information technology strategy.

In those cases where the purpose is more broadly defined, overall strategy will consist of a balanced and integrated set of strategies which reflect the need to serve quite disparate interests. Thus there will be a business strategy designed to achieve the desired level of return on shareholders' funds, a human resource strategy designed to maximize employee commitment and competence, a strategy for maximizing customer satisfaction, a strategy for building relationships with suppliers and a strategy for winning a favourable reputation in the community at large. A balanced approach of this kind is characteristic of several highly regarded companies such as Marks & Spencer and Shell.

ORGANIZATION

The word organization is used in two distinct ways in the English language. In one sense it is used to describe a complete social institution which has been deliberately created in order to serve some purpose. Institutions such as business enterprises, charities, government departments and universities are all 'organizations' in this usage and are thus differentiated from other forms of social grouping such as crowds, communities, age groups or social classes.

The second sense of the word occurs when it is used to describe the internal arrangements, relationships and processes which exist inside social institutions.

As we saw in the previous chapter, a widely accepted way of describing these internal arrangements is to group them under three headings: structure; systems and processes; and culture.

An organization is a 'whole' which in the last analysis defies our attempts to break it down into its component parts. Structure, systems and procedures and culture are all aspects of the same entity. They interact in complex ways and changes in one area have repercussions for the others.

THE CONDITIONS FOR ORGANIZATIONAL CHANGE

The circumstances which call for organizational change in the sense of changes in the internal arrangements of a social institution are as follows:

1. *A change of purpose*. In this set of circumstances the need arises for the business or public sector body to re-think its purpose and to set a new direction. This process will in turn lead to the need for a fresh approach to strategy and, in consequence, changes in organization so as to align it with the new purpose and new strategy.

   A common example of this in recent years is the process of privatization. As an organization moves from the public to the private sector its *raison d'être* undergoes radical change. On the one hand, however broadly the purpose may now be defined, the need to satisfy the demands of the stock market inevitably calls for new strategic thinking. On the other hand now that purpose is no longer so strictly defined by Act of Parliament many previous restrictions on the scope of the organization's activities are removed and it becomes possible to consider a much wider range of strategies such as acquisitions or diversification. If the privatization process is accompanied by deregulation, as in the case of the telecommunications industry, the organization must reach decisions about its competitive positioning. A national health hospital which elects for Trust status cannot escape rethink-

51

ing its purpose and its strategy. All these changes have obvious implications for organization.

The British Telecom case (Chapter 9) illustrates this situation very well.

2. *A change in strategy*. In these circumstances the organization's purpose remains but top management takes the view that it is necessary to rethink the strategy. A well-documented case is that of the Ford Motor Company. Starkey and McKinlay[4] have described how for many years this organization pursued a business strategy characterized by strong financial controls and a contractual (and often confrontational) relationship with its shop-floor employees.

> In the 1980s Ford Motor Company in the US negotiated what was one of the most spectacular turnarounds of all time, coming from the verge of extinction to the position of industry leader on a variety of performance indicators. At the core of this turnaround was a searching re-analysis of corporate strategy grounded in a successful attempt to come to terms with Fordism, undoing its constraints, confirming its strengths, all the while redefining management practices at Ford in a radically new way. At the heart of Ford's transformation in the US was the development of a new approach to the management of its human resource. The new approach emphasized employee involvement and employee participation, key elements of the emerging HR agenda.

This radical shift of strategy inevitably resulted in radical changes to the structure, systems and culture of the organization. This type of organizational change is exemplified by the Alliance & Leicester case (Chapter 9).

3. *The search for more effective organization*. The third set of circumstances exists in cases where top management sees no reason to redefine purpose, or to rethink the strategy, but does believe that the existing organization is ineffective in implementing and delivering the strategy.

There are some obvious examples where this set of circumstances applies.

One is the case in which the successful strategic management of the business in the context of a given purpose has led to considerable growth and/or diversification. The situation has been changed by the very success of the strategy and the organization must now be adapted to the greater size and complexity of the enterprise.

Another example results from the intensification of competition on the impact of new entrants to the market. A company seeking to maximize return on capital employed by positioning itself as the lowest cost producer in a given market may find its prices being undercut by a new entrant or by an existing competitor which has become more efficient at controlling costs. Such a company will tend to keep to its purpose and stick with its competitive strategy, seeking to re-establish itself as the lowest cost producer by such organizational changes as streamlining its structure or improving its production procedures and cost control systems.

LINKING STRATEGY WITH ORGANIZATION DESIGN

The Case of 'Carling Tools'

In an article in *Long Range Planning*, Douglas Cowherd and Robert Luchs[5] present the case of 'Carling Tools' (not its real name), a highly profitable producer of power tools in North America. At the time of the case the company held the second largest market share but there were some early warning signs of trouble ahead. Share was falling and competitors were becoming more innovative in both modifying existing products and launching new ones.

The management sought the help of consultants from the Strategic Planning Institute to help them find answers to the following critical questions:

○ Is the business secure?

○ If not, what needs to be done strategically and tactically?

○ What organizational changes should be undertaken to support the business strategy?

In seeking answers to these questions use was made of a database known as OASIS (Organization and Strategy Information Service) which had been set up in 1984 as a joint venture between Hay Management Consultants, the Strategic Planning Institute and the University of Michigan. A key objective of this database was to identify relationships between organizational variables and strategic success.

The analysis of Carling's situation in the light of OASIS data highlighted a number of important facts.

The business performance, with a return on investment (ROI) of 46 per cent, was excellent. This above-average rate of return reflected Carling's continuing ability to command premium prices for its products because of a long history of superior design features (differentiation through *perceived* quality). In recent times, however, Carling had fallen behind its competitors in terms of innovation. The indications were that failure to address this problem would result not only in continued loss of market share but in shrinking margins, etc. The key to success lay in closing the innovation gap, coupled with more effective marketing.

This diagnosis of the company's basic strategic weakness set the scene for a review of the organization. A comparison with the OASIS benchmarks for the number of levels in the hierarchy showed excess layers of management, particularly in marketing, which were contributing to Carling's slow response time. The business unit size (at 10,000 employees) was also too large for a quick response to the market-place. 'Shielded from direct contact with the market by the over-layered bureaucracy, top managers spent most of their time in financial and administrative activities while devoting little effort to sales and marketing.[5]

It was also judged that Carling's culture was a contributory factor to the problem. A culture survey revealed a culture characterized by little freedom for independent action, strong emphasis on formal procedures and little openness to change.

In sum the analysis concluded that a major change in organization was needed. Specific changes recommended were:

○ The business should be broken up into several smaller units.

○ Some middle management layers should be removed.

○ Some managers from outside should be brought in at top level.

○ Incentive reward systems should be revised and related more closely to business growth.

○ The chief executive should begin a process of changing the culture of the company with the aims of increasing levels of autonomy, informality and information.

These recommendations were accepted.

INCREMENTAL VERSUS TRANSFORMATIONAL CHANGE

When one examines case histories of organization change it is evident that there are important differences in the magnitude of the change which takes place as well as differences in the time-scale over which organizational change is spread.

Taking the two variables – the magnitude of the change and the time-scale involved – it is possible to identify four types of organizational change, as shown in Figure 3.1.

1. *Incremental or evolutionary change* consists of an ongoing process of moderate but linked steps none of which is particularly significant in itself, but which taken together result in sufficient adaptation to changed business conditions or modifications to strategy to enable the organization to remain effective. The starting point for such an approach usually involves a combination of satisfaction with past success and a realization that the world is changing and that only by a continuous process of organization change can future success be assured. Thus this process is seen as one which has no time limits – it will go on as long as the organization exists but, provided nothing happens to create a deep sense of crisis, it need never be traumatic.

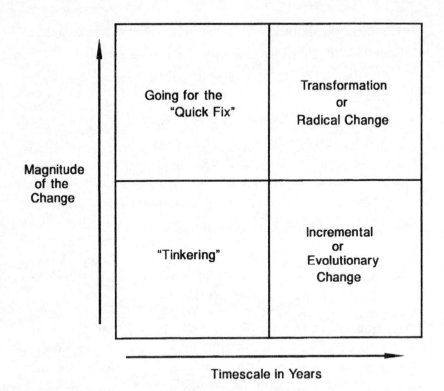

Figure 3.1   Four types of organizational change

2. *Transformational or radical change,* by contrast, is extremely traumatic. It is seen as necessary either in response to a severe crisis in the organization's affairs or a fundamental change in purpose or strategy. It involves challenging all the assumptions underlying existing organization arrangements and it results in changes so profound that after the event the organization is scarcely recognizable compared with its previous condition. Such a transformation takes years to work through – at least three and perhaps as many as seven. It cannot take place without significant and painful changes in culture. It is, however, limited in time. Once the transformation is complete the organization can either revert to a process of continuous incremental change or, exhausted by the turmoil of radical change, it may sink into a period of inertia and stagnation which in the end will necessitate a further bout of transforma-

tion. Transformational change is quite often achieved following a management buy-out. This is what happened in Fermec and the process is described in Chapter 9.

3. Attempts at achieving organizational transformation in a short time period – a year or so – are doomed to fail. However attractive the third option of a *quick fix* may appear (and in companies in deep crisis the appeal is obvious) the long-established and deeply entrenched patterns of organizational behaviour which prevail cannot be uprooted and displaced by short-term panaceas. It is like weeding the garden by pulling off the heads of the weeds. For a short while things look just fine but all too quickly the weeds are there just as thick as before. Frequently the quick fix approach involves implementing a 'package' of some kind which has an impressive label and which is being promoted by expensive teams of consultants. Sometimes these approaches fail because they focus on only one aspect of the total organizational nexus – the structure or the systems or the culture.
    Colin Marshall[6] speaking to a meeting of the Royal Society of Arts in 1990 made the point as follows:

    > We may be able to alter fashions, modes, practices and even basic thinking. However, if we accomplish no basic shift in values, if we confuse appearance with reality, then over the long-term, we will accomplish no real change in the culture at all.

    > To speak of a quick culture change is almost an oxymoron.

    > Management cannot allow itself to be fooled by what seem to be initially favourable results. It has to accept the fact that it is a long, continuing, arduous and expensive task which can be successful only if everyone concerned stays involved for the necessary span of time.

    > At British Airways I think that we have started to achieve true culture change. There are different perceptions of values and attitudes than there were seven years ago.

    As Ralph Kilman of the Forum consulting group points out[7]

    > It is time to stop perpetuating the myth of simplicity. The system of organization invented by mankind generates

complex problems that cannot be solved by simple solutions. The only alternative is to develop a truly integrated approach – a complete programme for managing today's organization. Complete programmes, however, are often preached but seldom practised.

4. The fourth box in the diagram is labelled *tinkering*. This describes the process of making occasional unrelated relatively minor organization changes in the hope or belief that they will lead to improved performance. For example a company might decide to introduce performance related pay in one year, then in the next year turn its attention to trying to improve quality without linking the issue of quality to the nature of the remuneration system. Organizations which tinker typically go through cycles – centralization followed by decentralization followed by re-centralization, etc.

All we were doing was going round in circles, constantly making changes, searching for the structure, then changing yet again.

Personnel Director IT Consultancy

PROACTIVE AND REACTIVE CHANGE

Most organizational change consists of a reaction to some other event or situation, be it privatization, financial crisis, merger or whatever. Examples of proactive change are harder to find. Proactive change involves anticipation of the need to change. It results from a high degree of sensitivity to changes in the environment or the ability to pick up early warning signals of problems on the horizon.

Table 3.1 shows the financial results of the US earthmoving equipment manufacturer Caterpillar for the years 1976 to 1988.

The year of record profit in 1981 was followed by a series of disastrous years which severely threatened the company's prospects for survival. When was the time to make changes? They actually began to take place in 1983, but 1980 and 1981 were the years when they were most needed and when they might have prevented the subsequent losses.

Table 3.1   Caterpillar's tracks

Year	Profit (loss) after tax ($ millions)
1976	383
1977	445
1978	566
1979	492
1980	565
1981	579 (record)
1982	(180)
1983	(345)
1984	(428)
1985	198
1986	76
1987	350
1988	616

Obviously, proactive change has much to commend it. Why, then, does it not happen more often? There are two reasons. First, companies rarely have information systems which help them tell where they are heading as distinct from logging where they have been. No doubt there was information somewhere in the system which would have indicated to Caterpillar's top management that things were not quite as rosy as they seemed on the surface. The kind of information that would be relevant would include increased stocks, loss of some key accounts, increased borrowing, loss of some key personnel, etc. Yet the implication is that either the Caterpillar management wasn't getting such information or, if receiving it, wasn't acting on it.

The second reason is that when things appear to be going well and companies are profitable it is extremely difficult to get people excited about change, given that they cannot see the need for it.

HOW ORGANIZATIONAL CHANGE AFFECTS PEOPLE

Organizations are populated by human beings and organizational change, far from being an abstract concept, has very real effects on people's lives.

The following are among the most common consequences of organizational change as it affects people.

1. *Redundancy*. Sadly, in many organizations, organizational change has become synonymous with job losses. When this has happened getting people to co-operate enthusiastically with change programmes has been likened to getting turkeys to vote for Christmas. There is, however, a world of difference between the call for voluntary redundancies on generous terms following full consultation with the employee groups involved, as in the case of British Telecom, described in Chapter 9, and the abrupt announcement of compulsory redundancies with only the statutory minimum compensation, particularly if the plant concerned is situated in an area of high unemployment. Given an increasingly competitive environment coupled with technological progress it is likely that in most industries productivity growth will outstrip output growth leading to a continued requirement to shed staff. When this is done through intelligent forward planning the slack can be taken up by natural wastage and voluntary redundancy, thus avoiding damaging the morale of the workforce.

2. *Changes in job content*. When jobs are redefined a wide range of consequences result. For some people it means loss of traditional craft skills. For others it means having to acquire new skills, having to work with new technology, having to be re-trained. It is all too easy to overlook the traumatic effects of such changes. The range of emotions that can

be set in train include anxiety about one's ability to master new skills, resentment at being 'sent back to school', loss of esteem and self-respect when traditional skills are no longer needed, and deep feelings of insecurity as people's sense of ownership of their jobs is undermined.

3. *Changes in social groupings*. The restructuring of organizations frequently results in the re-drawing of group boundaries, the breaking up of existing work groups and the formation of new ones. People have to adjust and build new relationships, re-establish feelings of mutual trust and a sense of group cohesion. New teams take time to settle in. While this is happening performance may deteriorate rather than improve.

4. *Changes in status*. All hierarchical systems of organization are status systems as well as systems for the allocation of authority and responsibility. Structural change virtually always results in unanticipated changes to people's status. Few changes are resisted more fiercely and few subjects arouse as much emotion. Anxiety about status is often a major factor in resistance to change but is difficult to resolve since it is usually unacknowledged. People will give any number of reasons for not going along with a set of proposed changes but keep quiet about the real reason – loss of status – since they will be reluctant to be open about this issue. This is partly because they do, indeed, feel somewhat ashamed to feel so deeply about the matter and partly because they would expect such feelings, however strong, to be given scant consideration by management.

5. *Loss of earnings or earnings potential*. In some instances organizational change threatens people's potential earning power – or may appear to do so. Examples include changes to production systems which eliminate the need for overtime working or changes to the system of remuneration which eliminate or modify rates for piece work.

6. *Changes in location*. Some organizational changes involve relocation of activities. People who are not being asked to accept redundancy may nevertheless be asked to move home

and family to an unfamiliar part of the country or even to another country altogether. Less dramatic moves may mean longer journeys to work.

7. *Changes in conditions of employment.* Under this heading falls a wide range of possible changes which affect individuals – changes in hours of work or in the system of shiftworking, changes in the method and frequency of payment, changes in the pension scheme, changes in the arrangements for claiming sickness benefit or changes in job grading systems.

8. *Changes in people's beliefs, values and assumptions.* Perhaps the most profound changes which affect individuals are among the least expected – changes in things like beliefs, values and assumptions. For example, changes in the financial services industries have led to a radically different approach to bank lending such that bank managers had to 'unlearn' their traditional caution and become aggressive salespeople. This change was not so much a change in skill as a change in basic assumptions and beliefs about banking and the role of the bank manager.

Similarly, people brought up in large public bureaucracies who were taught above all else to stick to the rules and who had seen risk-taking and discretionary behaviour dealt with punitively during their formative years have been required, post privatization, to operate flexibly, use judgement and take risks. Such changes turn peoples' values upside down.

When a chief executive alerts the organization to impending changes, people do not at first think about the consequences for the organization. Being human, they think first about the consequences for themselves. How will it affect me? Will I have to move? Will I still be working with my friends? Will I keep my place in the pecking order? If I have to be retrained, will I be able to cope? Questions such as these are at the heart of organization change. They are questions that make people's hearts beat faster, questions that are felt in the stomach rather than formulated in the brain.

References

1. Campbell, Andrew, Devine, Marion and Young, David (1990) *A Sense of Mission,* Economist Books/Hutchinson, London.

2. Royal Society of Arts (1994) *Tomorrow's Company: The Role of Business in a Changing World,* Interim Report, London.

3. Kotter, JP and Heskett, JL (1992) *Corporate Culture and Performance,* The Free Press, New York.

4. Starkey, Ken and McKinlay, Alan (1993) *Strategy and the Human Resource: Ford and the Search for Competitive Advantage,* Blackwell Business, Oxford.

5. Cowherd, Douglas and Luchs, Robert 'Linking organization structures and processes to business strategy', *Long Range Planning* Vol 21 No 5 October 1988.

6. Marshall, Sir Colin 'Culture change. No science but considerable art', *Journal of the Royal Society of Arts* January 1991.

7. Kilman, Ralph (1986) *Beyond the Quick Fix,* Jossey Bass, San Francisco.

4

Understanding Corporate Culture

INTRODUCTION

Culture was defined in Chapter 2 as 'an amalgam of shared values, a common "mindset", characteristic behaviours and symbols of various kinds.' Before a culture can be changed the first step is to create a clear picture and full understanding of the existing culture. This understanding should begin by developing insight into its origins.

In most organizations which have been in existence for any length of time the culture will almost certainly have developed in an unplanned, unconscious way, in that the values were never written down, the common assumptions were unspoken and taken for granted, and the characteristic behaviours were passed from one role model to another without deliberate attempts to create a pattern. Only in exceptional cases such as IBM and Hewlett Packard did the founder or founders set out quite consciously to create an organization with a distinctive culture from the outset.

THE ROOTS OF CULTURE

The roots of corporate culture are many and complex, including the following:

1. *The geographical origins of the parent company* which will bring influences from particular national or regional cultures.

Japanese and US firms differ among themselves but nevertheless show very strongly the influence of their respective national cultures.

2. *The traditional sources from which the senior managers have been drawn* – from the older universities, the 'redbrick' universities, private schools, from the shop floor, from the armed services, etc.

3. *The nature of the organization's core activity*. Heavy industry, dirty or dangerous work will breed quite different sets of values and assumptions from those which develop in such diverse industries as banking, fashion, entertainment or retailing. This reflects the different skills and qualities associated with success and thus the value placed on these skills and qualities.

4. *The organization's history*. In particular, culture will have been influenced by such things as:

   a) The organization's past record of achievement. Has consistent success bred complacency? Has frequent reversal of fortunes led to ingrained pessimism or a gritty determination to survive?

   b) What have business conditions been like? Monopoly, oligopoly or fierce competition? Exposure to market forces or cocooning within the public sector? Operating in stable markets or ones characterized by frequent innovation?

   c) The mark left on the organization by key figures from the past. These are often legendary and stories about them are passed on from one generation to another. The culture of the BBC, for example, is rich with stories and anecdotes about its founding Director General, Lord Reith.

5. *The organization structure and the systems and procedures in use*. As I pointed out earlier these aspects of the total organization interact with culture. They influence it and in turn are influenced by it.

NON-ADAPTIVE CULTURES

As the business environment grew increasingly turbulent in the 1970s and 1980s many large UK companies faltered or foundered because they could not adapt sufficiently quickly to the challenge of intensified global competition. Mostly these were organizations which were founded in the 19th or early 20th centuries and which had passed their formative years in a social, economic, political and technological setting very different from that which they were now experiencing.

These conditions included:

1. A society characterized by considerable emphasis on differences between the social classes and in particular between those who worked with their hands (blue-collar workers) and those who, even at relatively low skill levels such as clerks and typists, worked with their brains. It was taken for granted that 'staff' and 'hourly paid' should be treated differentially, with different hours and conditions of work, different degrees of job security, different places to eat, even different entrances to the buildings.

2. A highly protected home market, supplemented by Commonwealth preference, that made it possible to avoid serious competition through a combination of cartels and various non-tariff barriers.

3. A national culture in which careers in industry and callings such as engineer or chemist were looked down upon relative to careers in academe, the Church, the civil service or callings such as the professions of law and medicine.

4. A cultural setting in which women were expected to focus their lives and energies on the home. Those who sought employment were offered a narrow range of acceptable roles – teacher, nurse, secretary, shop assistant or assembly worker in light industry.

5. Relatively stable technologies and relatively slow rates of new product innovation. In the adaptive corporation, for

example, Alvin Toffler[1] points out that from its origins until 1954 the US corporation AT&T produced just one product – a standard black telephone. By the early 1970s, however, the company was producing some 25,000 different service options and 1500 types of telephone.

6. A world in which consumers were expected to be easily satisfied (and usually were) and in which to complain about poor service or product quality was taken as a sign of bad manners. A world in which a chronic inability to satisfy potential demand was intensified by acute shortages in two world wars, creating a climate in which customers were expected to wait patiently in queues and suppliers developed a 'take it or leave it' attitude.

7. An intellectual climate for management largely set by the work of Frederick W Taylor and his followers[2]. Taylor's work was based on the assumption that workers were both stupid and lazy. He argued that manual and mental work should be separated. Management, he claimed, should specialize in planning and organizing and workers should simply obey instructions. He also emphasized the advantages of making individuals specialize in relatively simple repetitive tasks in which they would become highly efficient. He advocated breaking complex jobs down into much simpler component parts, establishing the one best way of performing each part, studying the layout of the workplace and the design of tools and equipment so as to eliminate unnecessary actions or movement and selecting and training employees to use the one best way. 'Taylorism', as his approach became known, was responsible for much of the alienation and apathy in the workforce which was characteristic of Western manufacturing industry for many years and is so well captured in Huw Benyon's *Working for Ford*[3].

This environment led to the development of some common cultural characteristics in many large UK companies which made it very difficult for them to adjust to the social, economic, political and technological forces for change in the 1970s and 1980s.

The main features of this characteristic culture were:

1. *Complacency tinged with arrogance*. Past prosperity, market domination and a powerful reputation and image combined to breed the attitude that there was nothing left to learn.

2. *Conservatism*. A tendency to cling to the known and tried paths which had led to success in the past. A reluctance to experiment or take risks.

3. *A production-orientation*. These companies were slow to understand the role of marketing. Their focus was an internal one – on what it suited them to produce – rather than on customer needs and expectations.

4. *Bureaucracy*. This showed itself in huge head-offices (at one time ICI's corporate head office in Millbank House was known as Millstone House), cumbersome procedures and a tendency to treat the rules as ends in themselves rather than as means to an end.

5. *Personnel policies which were demeaning, divisive and confrontational*. Personnel management was seen largely as an administrative function having no strategic importance and thus not warranting a place on the board.

6. *Elaborate status systems* in which dining areas, company cars, parking places, even secretaries, were allocated in relation to a highly formal and elaborate pecking order.

7. *A secretive climate* which closely guarded information, particularly financial information, treating it as a source of power and control.

8. *A man's world* – virtually no women in very senior positions.

A look at the *Times* top 200 companies in 1974 (20 years ago) shows many names which no longer feature – companies which fell by the wayside principally because they had developed many of these cultural characteristics and, because these things had become so deeply rooted, were incapable of changing radically enough in the time available. Among the most well-known casualties were Imperial Tobacco, Dunlop and the Rootes Group.

How Cultures are Perpetuated

Kotter and Heskett[4], in their comprehensive study of corporate culture and its relationship with business performance in US firms, list several ways in which corporate cultures are perpetuated:

1. Through the process of personnel selection – choosing people who 'fit'.
2. During the induction process – passing on both formal and informal aspects of expected attitudes and behaviours.
3. By handing down legends and stories from the past and relating the words and deeds of heroic figures.
4. By the way influential members of the organization at all levels 'act out' the culture and serve as role models.
5. By the continuous communication of values, principles, beliefs, etc. It is common practice to have these printed on plastic cards and issued to all employees.
6. By rewarding behaviour which is consistent with the culture and doing so openly and publicly.

CULTURAL TYPOLOGIES

Charles Handy[5] and Roger Harrison[6] have both put forward the idea of typologies of organizational cultures.

Handy's four culture types are:

○ the role culture;
○ the power culture;
○ the person culture;
○ the task culture.

The Role Culture (or Bureaucratic Culture)

This is found more often in the public sector than in business. Bureaucracies work well under some conditions, such as a stable environment and a highly routine, standardized task such as issuing driving licences. In industry, large bureaucratic organizations developed in the era of mass production and in the commercial field in organizations like insurance companies when they employed armies of clerks. The values of the role culture – rationality, order, integrity, service efficiency, conformity and seniority – unite people in a common concern for doing things right, but not necessarily in doing the right things.

The Power Culture

Rather like a spider's web the power culture is dominated by a powerful individual at the centre who controls all resources and takes virtually all decisions. Organizations with such cultures can achieve outstanding performance for a time – as long as the source of power has a strong sense of direction, exercises sound judgement, makes the right decisions, behaves with integrity and wins loyalty from others.

Examples of such a figure were the late Lord Robens when chairman of the National Coal Board, or Sir Denis Rooke when chairman of British Gas. Where some of these vital elements are missing, however, the result can be disastrous, as was the case with the business empire controlled by the late Robert Maxwell. A weakness of power cultures is that they tend to lose their most able people who become frustrated at their lack of involvement in key decisions, leaving weaker, sycophantic executives to play the role of courtier.

The Person Culture

In this culture the individual is paramount and the organization structure and systems, insofar as they exist, are designed to facilitate and support the work of the key individual wealth earners. Such cultures exist in partnerships – law firms, medical practices and professional partnerships. Problems arise when these become very large as is the case, for example, with some accountancy practices. The result can border on anarchy.

The Task Culture

In such organizations power is widely distributed and is based upon expertise or competence rather than charisma or the holding of a particular office. The values will include achievement, teamwork, openness and trust, autonomy, personal growth and development. It is an adaptive culture, responsive to fresh ideas and new needs. It is well suited to a highly educated, intelligent workforce such as is found in a research and development organization. It is also appropriate in service organizations in which front-line service personnel need to be able to provide a flexible response to customers.

It is characteristic of task cultures to employ structural devices such as project teams or task forces and to operate with relatively flat structures.

Roger Harrison suggests a very similar typology and uses the terms *role culture*, *power culture*, *support culture* and *achievement culture* to describe four basic types.

Other types of business culture which do not fit neatly into these typologies are the entrepreneurial culture and the family business culture.

Entrepreneurial cultures are often characterized by a mix of the power and achievement cultures. They are by definition young organizations, lively and exciting places to work. The founder entrepreneur may be autocratic but is often benevolent and in any case has no shortage of followers – people who admire his/her innovative and risk-taking qualities. Richard Branson's Virgin organization is an outstanding example of this kind.

Family business cultures may also have some elements in common with the power culture. In these organizations there are two clearly separate sub-cultures – members of the family and the rest. Although such businesses may be extremely up to date in many respects they tend to retain some traditional practices, to be paternalistic towards employees and to cultivate a family atmosphere. The Morgan car company, which featured in the BBC series *The Troubleshooters*, is a good example of such a family business culture.

'Success' Cultures

Kotter and Heskett[7] looked at corporate culture and related it to performance in 207 US firms drawn from 22 industries. Using a simple questionnaire they constructed an index of 'cultural strength' for most of the companies and identified those with particularly 'strong' cultures. These had explicit statements of values and characteristic ways of doing things, and included such well-known cases as Wal-Mart, IBM, and Johnson and Johnson. They also identified a similar number with 'weak' cultures including Unisys, Control Data and Honeywell. They found a positive relationship between strength of culture and long-term business performance but the relationship was a modest one. They found a stronger relationship in the case of firms with 'strategically appropriate' cultures – ones in which the *content* was as important as the strength and there was a good fit between the culture and the strategy the firm was pursuing. The strongest relationship, however, was found in the case of companies with *adaptive* cultures. These, as mentioned in Chapter 3, were ones which emphasized their obligations to all the stakeholders. They were also distinctive in that their top executives acted as leaders rather than as managers.

GAINING INSIGHT INTO CULTURE

An approach which is simple in the extreme but nevertheless quite effective is to get a group of managers together and show them a list of descriptions of corporate culture similar to the one shown below. They are then asked individually and without discussion to write down their three adjectives they feel are most descriptive of their organization as it is at present.

Then they are asked to write down the three terms which, they feel, describe the culture that needs to be developed if the organization is to achieve its strategic aims.

The facilitator then enables the first set of adjectives to be shared and discussed. (On a recent occasion, of 24 very senior executives from a well known but struggling Plc, 23 listed 'conservative' first as a description of their company.) A similar process is followed with the second set of adjectives. The participants in the activity are then divided into small groups to discuss and resolve any areas of disagreement and to begin to think about how the organization can move from the first set of cultural characteristics to the second.

HOW PEOPLE DESCRIBE ORGANIZATIONS

adhocracy	hardworking
anarchic	hard drinking
authoritarian	innovative
bureaucratic	inward looking
caring	learning
competitive	macho
conservative	meritocratic
creative	militaristic
divisive	open
elitist	participative
egalitarian	paternalistic
entrepreneurial	political
'fat cats'	production oriented
fire-fighting	risk-avoiding
flexible	secretive
formal	technocratic
friendly	traditional
hierarchical	work hard/play hard

Edgar Schein, author of *Organizational Culture and Leadership*[8], suggests the following procedure for developing a deep understanding of an organization's culture:

1. Identify what he calls 'the cultural artifacts'. These are directly observable things and behaviours.

2. Identify the organizations espoused values – the things it states that it places a high value on.

3. Identify the underlying assumptions. This is the most difficult aspect since these are often unconsciously held and difficult to surface.

4. Check for strong sub-cultures which may be particularly proactive or defensive in respect of a particular set of changes.

He exemplifies what he means by cultural artifacts by describing the observable elements of culture in the 'Multi' company (a disguised multi-national based in Switzerland, producing chemicals and health care products, formed by a merger of two other companies some years previously).

The 'cultural artifacts' in this case included such things as keeping office doors closed, with red and green lights to indicate whether or not visitors would be received; an executive dining-room serving first-class food and wine; people addressing each other formally, using titles; no female senior managers; sticking rigidly to the chain of command; showing deference to those in higher authority; and elaborate planning processes.

Adjectives which would apply to a culture with such features would perhaps include:

O authoritarian;

O bureaucratic;

O conservative;

O elitist;

O formal;

O hierarchical;

O paternalistic;

O risk-avoiding;

O secretive;

O technocratic;

O work hard/play hard.

The 'Cultural Web'

Gerry Johnson and Kevan Scholes[9] have developed an approach which they have described as the 'cultural web'. They point out that the frames of reference (or paradigms) which managers develop over time are hedged about by different aspects of culture.

These include:

O the rituals of organizational life which accompany events such as training programmes, promotions, retirements, management or sales conferences, etc;

O the stories, myths and legends which get passed on to new recruits;

O symbols such as offices, logos, titles in use;

O the systems of measurement and the rewards system which together signify what the organisation regards as important;

○ the loci of power – for example are the marketing people most powerful or the accountants?;

○ the formal organization structure.

They give as an illustrative example the cultural web of a major UK clearing bank in the mid 1980s which is reproduced here, with permission, in Figure 4.1.

Johnson and Scholes suggest that the cultural web is a useful tool for analyzing the culture of a particular organization.

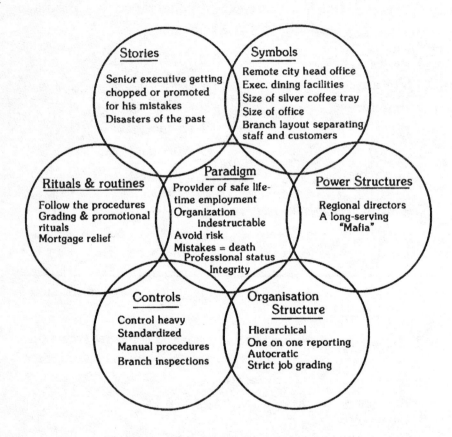

Figure 4.1 The cultural web of a UK bank in the 1980s
Source: Johnson and Scholes (1993) *Exploring Corporate Strategy*, (3rd edition). Reproduced by permission of the publisher, Prentice Hall International.

EXAMPLES OF CULTURE CHANGE

ICL

After ICL's takeover by STC in 1984 Peter Bonfield became managing director. He had worked closely with his predecessor, Robb Wilmot, who saw that the new business strategies essential for survival would require a fundamental change in the attitudes and values of employees. The changes would need to involve everybody. The objective was to be achieved with the aid of a 'cultural blueprint', a document defining seven commitments to be made by all staff and a further 10 obligations for all managers, providing a framework against which management performance could be measured. This document was *The ICL Way*, and its sub-title *The way we do things around here*. Ten years later this document remains the company's key statement about its culture and has wide acceptance among employees as a code by which to conduct themselves at work and to guide them in their relationships, both internal and external[10].

ROVER GROUP

At Rover it became clear that the objective of building a more open culture was incompatible with existing terms and conditions of employment for shop-floor employees. In consequence a set of changes known as 'Rover tomorrow, the new deal' was introduced[11]. The new conditions included:

○ no clocking;

○ single status;

○ merging hourly-paid and staff grading structures;

○ employment security;

○ devolution of authority to work teams;

○ a single joint negotiating committee representing all the recognized trade unions.

HAMPSHIRE COUNTY COUNCIL[12]

In local government the county surveyors' department of Hampshire County Council developed a planned programme of cultural change with the objective of moving from a traditional local authority department structured into separate professional groups to a business-oriented organization based on multi-disciplinary teams and with a strong sense of customer service. The 'trigger for change' was the appointment of a new county surveyor who provided the top management vision and leadership. He found a management board of five like-minded enthusiasts. This team developed a wide-ranging programme of changes involving organization structure, management style, values and training.

Nevertheless the principal focus was on culture and on achieving real change. The question arose: how well was the programme achieving this? Hence the decision to attempt to measure and monitor the extent of culture change. The idea of 'cultural snapshots' was then developed. These were to be built up by interviewing a cross-section of staff and supplementing the interview material by direct observation. This work was undertaken by an external organization development (OD) specialist.

In the interviews respondents were asked to describe their work, to talk about significant people in their work situations, and to describe typical work incidents. They were then invited to describe their department as they thought a visitor might see it. Finally they were asked to express their perceptions of the department by drawing pictures. The observation aspects of the study simply involved 'loitering with intent to understand what was going on'. One common feature to emerge from the first snapshot was that the department was seen by its staff as insular and compartmentalized. There was also some confusion about the department's primary objectives. Other perceived features of the existing culture included:

○ a concern with *maintenance*, ie keeping things going rather than changing direction;

○ strong valuation of professional qualifications;

○ a masculine department, not socially or professionally welcoming to women;

○ a philosophical resignation to poor office accommodation;

○ a mismatch between training aspirations and resources.

A second 'snapshot' 12 months later revealed a more positive feeling – a sense of going somewhere. Other features included a reduction in compartmental attitudes, a sense of a culture in transition but with managers changing faster than the rest, recognition of a change in management style, a general perception of being more business-like and customer-oriented, some sense of sadness for loss of separate professional identity on the part of staff in multi-disciplinary teams, a greater sense of ownership and of responsibility for one's own training and development, and a greater concern for performance management.

One vivid cultural picture was of a ship in a storm, with the crew working hard to keep the vessel afloat while the senior officers were up in the crow's nest proclaiming a vision on the far horizon.

Monitoring Culture Change

Frizzell Financial Services was one of the first organizations to use Saville & Holdsworth's corporate culture questionnaire to monitor progress in managing change[13].

This questionnaire, which was publicly launched in March 1994, asked employees to grade 126 statements about their organization on a scale ranging from 'strongly agree' to 'strongly disagree'. The issues raised included such topics as the workload, the level of bureaucracy, and the way customers are treated. The results were then grouped into 21 subject categories each of which was scored on a scale of 1 to 10, with a score of 5.5 representing the average score from all organizations involved in a three-year trial of the questionnaire.

Following changes to increase empowerment in pilot work-teams in Frizzell, the teams scored significantly higher than workers in traditional departments on a number of scales including 'job involvement', 'employee influence on decisions' and 'concern for the longer term'.

References

1. Toffler, Alvin (1985) *The Adaptive Corporation,* Gower, Aldershot.

2. Taylor, Frederick W (1911) *The Principles of Scientific Management,* Harper, New York.

3. Benyon, Hugh (1984) *Working for Ford,* Penguin Books, London.

4. Kotter, JP and Heskett, JL (1992) *Corporate Culture and Performance,* Free Press, New York.

5. Handy, Charles (1985) *Understanding Organizations,* Pelican Books, London.

6. Harrison, Roger (1987) *Organization Culture and Quality of Service,* AMED, London.

7. Kotter and Heskett, *op. cit.*

8. Schein, Edgar (1992) *Organizational Culture and Leadership,* Jossey Bass, San Francisco.

9. Johnson, Gerry and Scholes, Kevan (1993) *Exploring Corporate Strategy* (3rd edn), Prentice Hall, Hemel Hempstead.

10. Beattie, Don and Tampoe, FMK 'Human resource planning for ICL', *Long Range Planning,* Vol 23 No 1 February 1990.

11. Bower, David 'Becoming a learning organization – the experience of the Rover Group' in Philip Sadler (ed) (1993), *Learning More About Learning Organizations,* AMED, London.

12. Lisney, Bob and Allen, Cliff 'Taking a snapshot of cultural change', *Personnel Management* February 1993.

13. Reported in *Personnel Management* February 1993.

5

Preparing the Ground

CREATING A CLIMATE IN WHICH CHANGE IS ACCEPTED AS INEVITABLE

There are many well-documented examples of companies reaching the brink of disaster before the need for radical change was widely accepted. In the UK, ICL, ICI, Rover Group, British Airways and many others fall into this category, as do Caterpillar, Ford, Chrysler and IBM in the US. Ideally the need to change should be anticipated by top management and accepted by others well before the red ink starts to appear in the profit and loss account. In the UK, Bob Horton of BP set out to achieve this but lost his job in the process. In the US Jack Welch of GE is widely held up as the role model for bringing about radical change unaided by the pressures of imminent bankruptcy. This is an issue which John Harvey-Jones addresses in his book *Making it Happen*[1]. He emphasizes the need to build on the dissatisfaction with the status quo which comes from feeling threatened by the superior performance of others – other organizations, other countries, other products. He argues for a climate of openness in which the accounts are open to all so that every single employee knows whether the business is doing well or badly. Harvey-Jones concedes that to be able to communicate in the good times that although things are going well they need to be still better, is a very difficult task indeed. He points out, too, that it is in the companies which have been successful over many years that awareness of the need to change is most difficult to create.

One approach which he advocates is to alert people to the threat of competition by sending groups of managers and employees, including union representatives, on visits to competitors particularly in Germany, Japan and America. The very fact that such studies are very expensive helps indicate that top management are taking the problem very seriously indeed. Richard C Whitely[2] reports that Stew Leonard's famous supermarket in Norfolk, Connecticut owns a bus which is used to take groups of 12 employees at a time on field trips to other supermarkets up to 400 miles away. This procedure is known as the 'One Idea Club' – each person is asked to find one aspect in which the store being visited outperforms Stew Leonard's and suggest how the gap can be closed. Harvey-Jones also points to the important part played by the exercise of leadership, involving such things as understanding the human forces at work, sensitivity, patience, and example. He also underlines the symbolic importance of starting with changes which affect the top of the organization. In the case of ICI the way the board worked was radically changed and its size sharply reduced. The numbers in head office were cut from 1200 to around 400.

Two frequently used ways of drawing attention to the need for radical change are *benchmarking* and *surveys* – of customers, employees or both.

Benchmarking

Companies frequently settle into a state of complacency combined with arrogance because the performance data by which they judge themselves are internally focused and involve comparisons with their own past track record rather than with the best in the world currently. Even when external comparisons are readily available a form of organizational myopia develops which makes it very difficult to bring home the truth and the few people who try to do so make themselves very unpopular. The steps now being taken by British Telecom to reduce its staffing and make itself more domestically and internationally competitive (see Chapter 9) reflect the building up of such a state of complacency during its existence as a public sector monopoly.

ASKING THE RIGHT QUESTIONS

Some years before John Harvey-Jones was appointed chairman of ICI he had written and circulated a note entitled 'A Look at ICI in 1974'. This was circulated to the Board without being toned down, and produced an extremely strong reaction. Harvey-Jones recalled later how the chairman was 'white with rage'.

This is a typical response when someone has the courage to ask fundamental questions no matter how embarrassing they might be. When Harvey-Jones in turn became chairman he called a meeting of his fellow directors and asked them if ICI should be in chemicals anymore. The question produced a shock wave. Above all else it provoked people into doing some fresh thinking.

Source: Kevin Barham and Clive Rassam (1989) *Shaping the Corporate Future*, Unwin Hyman.

Benchmarking is a process which enables a company to make objective comparisons between its own performance and the best practice existing elsewhere. It is when the gaps between such best practice and the company's own standards are shown to be alarmingly wide that a climate receptive to change is established. Such comparisons should by no means be confined to one's own industry. Best practice with respect to particular operations may be found in a completely different type of business. The particular operations of greatest importance for benchmarking purposes are the *critical success factors*, which are those aspects of a company's operations which really make a difference and are the principal source of competitiveness.

The Xerox Corporation is frequently quoted as the first major First World company to initiate major change as a direct consequence of benchmarking. In the early 1980s they carefully examined how their Japanese competitors developed new products, how they made them and at what cost, how they distributed them, etc. The results were, indeed, alarming. Their product development cycle was twice as lengthy as that of the Japanese, used five times as many engineers, involved four times as many design changes and three times the design costs. Xerox also had over 30,000 defective parts per million compared with less than 1000 in the Japanese companies. The benchmarking process, as well as alerting members of an organization to the need for change, also points to meaningful change objectives. For example, in the case of Xerox above, such objectives included reducing the incidence of defective components to less than 1000 per million.

Surveys

Acceptance of the need for change can also be encouraged by carrying out surveys among relevant groups and publicizing the results. Complacency can be shattered by survey results which reveal significant customer dissatisfaction or which reveal the reasons why accounts have been lost to the competition.

Employee attitude surveys are particularly important when it is the management which most needs convincing of the need to change. Rover Group's first attitude survey in 1986 showed how the company's own systems and procedures, management style and practices were all creating barriers to the achievement of consistently high quality.

CREATING A POSITIVE THIRST FOR CHANGE

There is a world of difference between the attitude of mind which involves passive or indeed grudging acceptance of the need for change, and that which is fired with enthusiasm and which sees change as offering new opportunities and fresh horizons for the individual as well as timely renewal for the organization. Very high standards of leadership are, however, called for if such attitudes are to be fostered right through the organization. The processes involved are usually referred to as the creation of a shared vision and of a sense of mission.

Vision

Vision, in this context, is a description of a desired future state of the organization.

Whereas mission is about ultimate purpose, values and standards, vision is about what it is possible to achieve or what it is possible to become. It is usually used to refer to situations in which such a desired future state implies following a different path in the future from that which has proved successful in the past. The term contains the idea of innovative, imaginative thinking which challenges the conventional wisdom and points the way to new opportunities.

The development of a vision involves thinking freely without being constrained by the past or by current limitations to freedom of action. It is about 'dreaming ahead' as distinct from 'planning ahead'.

A vision acts as a beacon guiding travellers to their destination. In getting there it may be necessary to make a detour or retrace steps from time to time, but the vision is not lost sight of.

Prahalad and Doz[3] studied 16 cases of strategic redirection – some successful, some which failed and some where the jury was still out. They concluded that the appointment of a new key executive bringing a different vision was a necessary but not sufficient condition for success.

This point emphasizes how difficult it is to develop a radically new mindset or paradigm in a situation in which one's thinking is constrained by familiarity. The newcomer is not only likely to bring a fresh approach, he or she has no vested interest in, or protective feelings about, the existing order of things. When Sir Colin Marshall arrived at British Airways his ability to bring a new vision was not only a function of the fact that he came from a different industry and one in which service was paramount. It was also a function of the fact that he felt no ownership of BA's existing structure or culture and no sense of personal loyalty to those who had created them.

The exception to the rule that the visionary leader comes from outside the organization appears to be the visionary entrepreneur who builds an entire organization on the basis of a vision of what could be. Well-known examples include Ray Kroc the founder of McDonalds, Soichero Honda, and Richard Branson. These, however, are examples of a vision consistently pursued over many years as distinct from the achievement of radical strategic redirection.

It is certainly the case, however, that the vision must originate at, or very close to, the top of the organization. Beckhard and Pritchard[4] argue that the task of developing the *eventual* vision statement is a task for top management and one that cannot be delegated. Their emphasis on the word eventual implies that top management may first go through a consultative process, inviting ideas and suggestions from members of the organization. It is undoubtedly important that whatever process is chosen the vision should be widely owned and shared but there are obvious dangers in using a 'bottom up' approach. If the ideas forthcoming as a consequence of consultation are insufficiently radical or far-reaching then top management will have no choice but to discard them, in which case the consultation will be seen to have been a sham. The risk of such an outcome is quite high. Is it at all likely that British Airways' new vision would have emerged from such a procedure?

The alternative is for top management – usually the chief executive – to take the lead, develop a vision and seek subsequently to share it with others and to speed the ownership. To do this successfully calls for very considerable leadership skill.

In the early stages the vision is likely to be fragile and tentative. It will need refining, testing, and supporting with data if it is to become robust enough to withstand critical scrutiny and face opposition. Wise chief executives will first run their ideas by their top team, perhaps initially only with those whom they judge to be the more imaginative or adaptable among the team.

Assuming that this process does, indeed, strengthen the chief executive's conviction about the direction in which the organization needs to move, the further steps which may need to be taken include the following:

○ Create arenas or 'fora' within the organization at other levels in which possible alternative futures are discussed. In this way people will become accustomed to the process of challenging the conventional wisdom and current assumptions.

○ Take advantage of opportunities to meet members of the organization face to face and expose some of the new thinking.

When the time is ripe for the new vision to be 'launched' it must be presented so as to achieve the following:

○ It must be exciting, even inspiring.

○ It must 'feel right', leaving people feeling 'at last we know where we are going'.

○ It must be believable – something that people feel is within their grasp.

○ It should give at least some indications of how the vision is to be turned into reality.

To achieve all these things demands careful planning and preparation and highly professional standards of presentation. The chief executive should explain the vision personally to as many people as possible. The highest standards of audio-visual communication should be used in support. The vision should, if at all possible, be encapsulated in a few words.

G J Medley[5] has described how the new vision of the World-Wide Fund for Nature, UK, was developed by a team consisting of the director, the chief executive officer and the heads of the eight departments that reported directly to him. After reaching consensus on the issue of where the organization was currently, the group was divided into two teams and asked to answer the question 'What sort of an organization would you like to see WWF UK as being in five years' time?'. Each team began by developing lists of 'ideals'. What should the organization try to achieve? How should it be perceived? What sort of people should it employ? What activities should it engage in, etc? These ideas were then debated within each group until a consolidated answer was reached. The next stage was for the two groups to pool their ideas – which proved to be remarkably similar.

ENGLISH NATURE'S VISION STATEMENT

English Nature will take the lead in sustaining and enriching England's natural heritage for all to enjoy, now and in the future.

We will share our knowledge, understanding and practical experience to improve, enable and empower people to achieve this with us.

The service we deliver will be founded on a strategic approach to the conservation of wildlife and natural features.

Jack Welch – without doubt one of the world's most effective business leaders of the last 10 years – articulated his vision of General Electric in the following terms:

> A decade from now I would like General Electric to be perceived as a unique, high-spirited, entrepreneurial enterprise – a company known around the world for its unmatched level of excellence. I want General Electric to be the most profitable highly diversified company on the earth, with world-quality leadership in every one of its product lines.

Creating a Sense of Mission

Andrew Campbell and his colleagues[6] point out that many managers do not understand the nature and importance of mission while others fail to give any thought to it whatsoever. Part of the problem is that there is no generally accepted definition of what the term means.

Campbell distinguishes two schools of thought. One sees mission as a statement about business strategy while the other views mission as a matter of philosophy, values or even ethics.

In the first approach mission defines a company's commercial rationale, identifying the markets it serves and its goals in that context. It provides answers to such questions as 'What business are we in?' and 'What business should we be in, in X years' time?' This way of thinking, they suggest, owes its origin to a famous article which appeared in the *Harvard Business Review* in 1960 – 'Marketing myopia' by Theodore Levitt. He argued that most businesses defined their markets too narrowly. For example a railroad company should see its business as transporting people and goods, not just running train services. Similarly an oil company should see itself as in the energy business, and a business manufacturing tin cans as in the packaging industry.

Today it is common for companies to spell out their definition of their business in annual reports and promotional literature. Campbell quotes the following illustration from British Telecom's 1989 annual report.

> British Telecom's mission is to provide world class telecommunications and information products and services and to develop and exploit our networks at home and overseas.

The second school of thought, on the other hand, sees mission as a statement of the underlying values and beliefs which bind people together in common purpose. Campbell uses the term 'cultural glue' to express this idea. When used in this way mission constitutes an appeal principally to the emotions. Among the well-known businesses which have used mission in this way is IBM. Thomas J Watson junior, in his book *A Business and its Beliefs*, has described the company's basic values and argues that they were, for many years, the foundation of IBM's success.

The contribution of Campbell and his colleagues lies chiefly in the way they have brought these two approaches together. They argue that mission ideally should appeal both to the minds (strategy) and the hearts (cultural values) of the members of organizations. They point to successful companies such as Marks & Spencer, in which strong values are combined with a clear sense of strategic direction and purpose and in which people know what standards of behaviour are expected of them.

Their definition of mission involves four elements:

1. *Purpose*. What is the company for? For whose benefit is the effort being put in?

An excellent illustration here is the statement by George Merck, son of the founder of Merck, the world's largest pharmaceutical business: 'Medicine is for the patients. It is not for the profits'.

Many companies avoid making statements about purpose. Among those that do, Campbell identifies three sub-groups (identified previously in Chapter 3).

First, there are businesses which proclaim that they exist for the benefit of shareholders.

Secondly there are companies which take the inclusive approach and define their purpose in terms of meeting the expectations of the 'stakeholders' – employees, customers, suppliers and the community as well as the shareholders. Examples include BP and Sainsbury's.

Thirdly there are companies which have identified a purpose beyond the needs or expectations of the stakeholders. A much quoted example – but one which has not escaped scepticism about its sincerity – is Body Shop.

2. *Strategy*. Whatever the purpose, there is a need for a strategy which indicates how that purpose will be achieved.

Strategy defines the markets in which the business will operate and how it will build a competitive position.

3. *Behaviour standards*. Purpose and strategy are mere words unless they are translated into action. To do this involves identifying the standards of performance and the patterns of behaviour that will be required and taking steps to ensure that these are achieved in practice. In British Airways, for example, the purpose, as stated by Sir Colin Marshall, was to become 'the world's favourite airline' and 'to be the best and most successful company in the airline industry'. The strategy was to achieve this by providing superior service relative to the competition. Huge expenditure on training at every level from the board to the shop floor was then invested in training which both indicated the standards and behaviour patterns which would be required and provided the development of skills and competencies which these standards called for.

4. **Values**. Values are the underlying beliefs which give a moral force to the other aspects of mission. Values are, literally, the things people value. In British Airways, changing the values system involved getting people to place a higher value than in the past on such things as service standards and customer satisfaction.

The four elements are combined into what has become known as the Ashridge Mission Model (Figure 5.1). The diamond shape serves to remind us that a strong sense of mission exists when the four elements of mission reinforce each other.

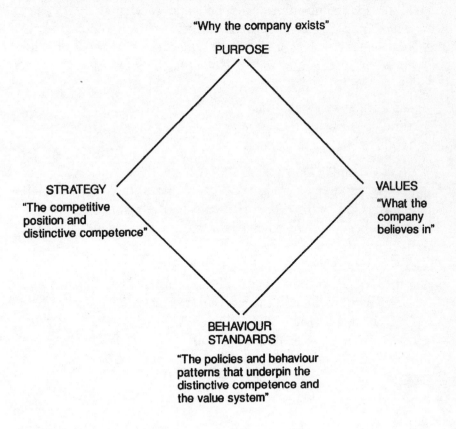

Figure 5.1 The Ashridge Mission model

Campbell makes some further valid points on the subject.

○ Working with an organization with a high moral purpose does not of itself mean that employees will have a strong sense of mission. Much depends on how far the individual's personal values and beliefs match those of the organization. It is evident from some recent worrying examples that not all employees in geriatric or mental hospitals have a strong sense of a mission involving care and consideration for patient well-being.

○ In order to promote a strong sense of mission careful recruitment is very important. Most people don't change their values when they join an organization and it is important to select people with values and beliefs which make a good fit with those of the organization, as Body Shop, for example, does.

○ Issuing a mission statement does not create a strong sense of mission. It involves much more – in particular it takes a long time to identify the appropriate behaviours and to set the required performance standards.

A good example of a mission statement is shown below. This is issued by Baxter, a large US-based healthcare business. It contains three of the four elements in the Ashridge model – Purpose (here referred to as primary objective), Values (referred to as principles) and Strategy. Although a statement of standards and behaviours is not included this does not mean that the company does not have them. They are usually too detailed and too lengthy to include in the mission statement.

One company which does clearly set out the behaviour standards it expects its managers to conform to is ICL. These are included in a carefully designed brochure called *The ICL Way*, a copy of which is given to each employee.

BAXTER'S MISSION STATEMENT

Mission: our primary objective

We will be the leading health care company by providing the best products and services for our customers around the world, consistently emphasizing innovation, operational excellence and the highest quality in everything we do.

Principles: what we stand for

We are committed to:

○ Customers: aggressively meeting customer needs.

○ Employees: respecting employees as individuals and providing opportunities for their personal development.

○ Stockholders: achieving long-term growth and the best return for our investors.

Through:

○ Teamwork: working strongly as a Baxter team.

○ Quality: reaching an objective understanding of customer requirements and using all our resources to satisfy those requirements.

○ Business excellence: acting ethically and continuously striving for excellence in our performance.

Strategy: the course we're taking

We are unique in our product and service breadth and our technological depth. We will use these strengths to:

○ Grow our business by providing the best quality in products and services to customers and to suppliers.

○ Provide products and services to deliver effective therapy to patients in lower cost settings, inside and outside the hospital.

○ Creatively apply technology to develop and maintain high-return leadership positions in selected markets worldwide.

○ Be the best cost producer by emphasizing innovative technology, cost and quality.

The 10 'obligations' of the ICL manager are as follows.

1. ***Business manager/people manager***. 'In our industry in particular managers must understand that profits are made by people, not by products. Consequently they must effectively manage, invest in and develop their people if they and ICL are to enjoy long-term success.'

2. ***Direction***. 'Managers must have detailed knowledge of ICL's objectives and strategies.'

3. ***Strategic thinking***. 'Managers are expected continually to identify future opportunities.'

4. ***High value outputs***. 'Achievement in ICL is all about output, not input or effort. More specifically it means high value output ... output that creates a demonstrable impact on our business results.'

5. ***Teamwork***. 'Success in a knowledge industry such as ours depends upon an effective sharing of the talent we have in the company.'

6. ***Development***. 'ICL is committed to developing its employees to the full extent of their potential.'

7. ***Can-do attitude***. 'ICL managers are required to set the pace and lead by example.'

8. ***Innovation***. 'It is the manager's obligation to set the framework for creativity.'

9. ***Difficult issues***. 'To ignore or hide problems is poor management. The ICL way is to confront and resolve them.'

10. ***Self-measurement***. 'Managers must continually challenge and appraise their own management actions... A manager must measure his own effectiveness as a people manager for his ability to provide leadership is particularly important.'

References

1. Harvey-Jones, John (1989) *Making It Happen*, Fontana/Collins, Glasgow.

2. Whiteley, Richard C (1991) *The Customer Driven Company,* Business Books, London.

3. Doz, Yves L and Prahalad, CK 'A process model of strategic re-direction in large complex firms: The case of multi-national corporations' in A Pettigrew (ed) (1988) *The Management of Strategic Change,* Basil Blackwell, Oxford.

4. Beckhard, Richard and Pritchard, Wendy (1992) *Changing the Essence,* Jossey Bass, San Francisco.

5. Medley, GJ 'WWF UK creates a new mission', *Long Range Planning* Vol 25 No 2 April 1992.

6. Campbell, Andrew, Devine, Marion and Young, David (1990) *A Sense of Mission,* Economist Books/Hutchinson, London.

6

Holistic Approaches – Total Quality and Business Process Re-Engineering

In recent years programmes of organizational change which aim to be transformational and which have an impact on virtually every aspect of organizational life have become widespread. In many cases the programmes are centred round a theme, are to some extent 'packaged', usually involve a role for external consultants, and reflect generally-accepted ideas about the factors which chiefly influence organizational performance. The two main approaches are Total Quality Management (TQM) and Business Process Re-engineering (BPR).

TOTAL QUALITY

Quality is far from being a novel idea. The concept of quality control entered into management thinking and practice in the 1930s. It found its expression mainly in two areas – inspection of finished products and statistical sampling. Two things have changed since then, both of which reflect the growing intensity of global competition and the related growth in the power of the consumer. The first is that quality has now become universally defined in terms of customer perceptions and expectations rather than in terms of production specifications as was the case in the past.

Secondly the *relative* importance of meeting customer requirements in terms of quality has increased in comparison with the

99

importance attached to other objectives such as cost control, growth in market share, or productivity. As the phrase Total Quality Management (TQM) implies, quality is now seen in many companies as the key issue to be addressed and as the chief driver behind programmes of organizational change.

One of the most successful quality 'gurus', Philip Crosby[1], has argued that the achievement of total quality requires the implementation of 14 actions, but not in sequence – most of them run in parallel. These are summarized below:

1. Demonstrate convincingly that top management is wholeheartedly committed to quality.
2. Set up a quality management task force representative of all functions and served by a full-time facilitator.
3. Decide how quality is to be measured.
4. Calculate the cost of quality.
5. Create widespread awareness (and excitement) through a wide range of media.
6. Take corrective action to eliminate problems permanently.
7. Make the commitment to zero defects.
8. Make the commitment public.
9. Educate all employees.
10. Set intermediate goals.
11. Encourage people to say what problems they are experiencing so that they can be tackled.
12. Provide recognition for those making the greatest contributions – preferably nominated by their peers.
13. Set up quality councils.
14. Do it all over again, as quality improvement is a continuous process.

Quality Circles

Most organizations which adopt a TQM approach to managing major organizational change set up teams of employees to discuss quality issues and make recommendations. Usually, but not always, these are called 'quality circles', which were first developed in Japan.

A circle normally consists of a group of between four and 12 people drawn from the same part of the company who voluntarily meet regularly to discuss work-related problems, particularly those to do with quality. Usually there is a steering group which oversees the whole process and in most cases the activity is supported by trained facilitators and/or circle leaders.

For quality circles to be effective the following conditions need to be present:

1. Commitment, support and interest from the top.

2. Co-operation and responsiveness from middle management.

3. Adequate preparation and training.

4. Adequate recognition and reward for success.

5. The company culture must be able to support a participative approach and the pre-existing climate of employee relations must be one of openness and trust. (For this reason quality circles failed to take root in Ford UK in the early 1980s.)

6. All parties must be patient and not expect miracles overnight.

7. Circle members need to be exposed to direct feedback from the customer. When successfully introduced the circles can act as powerful forces for change. They played a significant role in British Airways' transformation, where they were called 'Customer First Teams'.

BS 5750 and ISO 9000

The British Standards Institute (BS 5750) and the International Standards Organization (ISO 9000) offer quality standards accreditation systems which have been adopted by most firms following the Total Quality route. This approach has attracted some criticism on the grounds that the process is overly bureaucratic and that it focuses on internal definitions of quality rather than on customer needs.

Benchmarking

This technique also forms part of the TQM process in most cases. Its aim is to identify 'best practice' particularly in those aspects of the business which have been identified as critical success factors. The process breaks down into the following stages:

1. Deciding which processes to benchmark. This in turn means identifying the critical success factors which create and maintain customer satisfaction.
2. Developing accurate and objective descriptions of the existing processes.
3. Deciding which aspects to measure and how to measure them.
4. Choosing companies against which to benchmark.
5. Measuring the gap between the current standard and that of the best practice found elsewhere.
6. Implementation of findings to close the gap.

Benchmarking was discussed in some detail in the previous chapter.

Partnership with Suppliers

An important aspect of the overall change brought about by a TQM approach is a changed relationship with suppliers. The traditional 'antagonistic' approach, playing one supplier off against another and squeezing margins, may be capable of supporting a 'lowest cost' strategy but it does little for quality. To ensure adequate quality performance from bought-in materials and components calls for sustained collaborative relationships with suppliers, sometimes going as far as joint design engineering, joint planning and scheduling, and joint training. One example of this approach quoted by Matthyssens and Van den Bulte[2] is

ABB which distributes a brochure to its suppliers – 'ABB and its suppliers – expectations of the relationship'. It lists its expectations as 'error-free quality and delivery, compressed cycle times, reasonable prices, innovative engineering capability and a share of total cost improvements.'

In the UK, Marks & Spencer has long served as a model in this respect. It has developed very close relationships with its suppliers and employs large numbers of technical advisers to help them raise quality.

Quality Awards

In 1988 14 leading Western European companies formed the European Foundation for Quality Management. In 1991 the Foundation established the European Quality Award which is given annually to the most successful exponent of Total Quality Management in Western Europe. The European TQM model is shown in Figure 6.1. (The US equivalent is the Malcolm Baldrige award.)

TQM in Xerox

The Xerox story has been told by Robb Walker[3]. In 1980 Americans learned to their surprise that Japan's leading quality award was named after Dr W Edwards Deming, an eighty-year-old American statistician. Deming, together with another US consultant JM Juran, worked with Japanese companies in the 1950s helping them transform the quality of their products beyond all recognition. They advocated a mix of philosophy and powerful techniques, particularly statistical quality control. When US companies started to use the same approaches the results were dramatic. Xerox was an example. Its Japanese subsidiary began its quality improvement programme in 1976 under the theme 'New Xerox Movement' and won the Deming prize in 1980. In 1983 the Xerox Corporation initiated its Leadership Through Quality programme. Quality was defined as 'providing our internal and external customers with innovative products and services that fully satisfy their requirements'. Xerox's first step

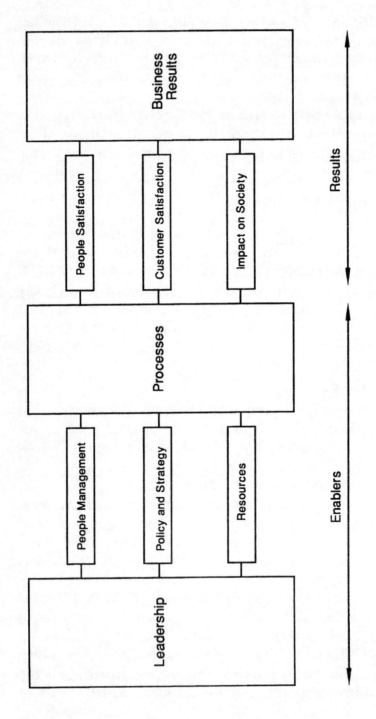

Figure 6.1 The European TQM model (European Foundation for Quality Management)
Source: European Foundation for Quality Management

was to institute competitor benchmarking – looking at how competitors developed their products, their cost structures, their distribution systems, and so on. Among the findings was the startling fact that Xerox was experiencing 30,000 defective parts per million compared with the Japanese figure of less than 1000.

At the heart of the change programme was a move away from a traditional 'command and control' structure with functional divisions and a steep hierarchy, to a much more cross-functional and participative organization in which teams and self-managed work groups featured strongly. Company objectives were redefined in terms of four priorities:

1. Customer satisfaction.
2. Employee satisfaction.
3. Return on assets.
4. Market share.

A strategy for the achievement of these aims was developed, involving six principles:

1. Customers define our business.
2. Success depends on the involvement and empowerment of highly trained people.
3. Line management is responsible for quality.
4. Management provides clear direction and objectives.
5. Strategic quality challenges are identified and met.
6. Business is managed and improved by using facts.

In addition, business process re-engineering was used to redesign all the key business processes.

Rank Xerox, the Xerox Corporation's UK subsidiary, won the European Quality Award in 1992.

TQM in Rover Group

David Bower[4] has described how Rover Group launched its Total Quality Improvement Programme in 1987.

The objective was to promote company-wide awareness of Total Quality Principles and to bring about the involvement of all employees in quality improvement activities.

The first phase involved major training programmes to promote awareness of TQI principles and the setting up of a 'quality leadership' structure within the company to carry the programme forward.

Including board members, 300 executives took part in four-day courses in 1987 and in the following two years 4000 managers and first-line supervisors received the same training. Courses were arranged as mixed function/mixed site groups of 15. The facilitators were managers on full-time secondment to the programme. All participants took on a quality improvement project at the end of the course, with feedback to a workshop six months later.

The training for all remaining employees, known as 'TQI cascade' was begun in January 1989 and completed within two years. Over 500,000 training hours were involved.

The quality leadership structure involved at top level a Quality Council which has met at quarterly intervals since mid-1987 to provide direction, guidance and policy. Individual Council members are also active in leading quality initiatives in their own areas of responsibility. Below this level a network of TQI steering groups was established.

At the operational level 500 'quality action groups' (directed by management) were set up as well as over 100 voluntary teams of shop-floor workers.

In 1989 the Council created the Rover Group Vision: 'To be internationally renowned for extraordinary customer satisfaction.'

TQM in ICL

ICL has consistently pursued quality improvement since the mid-1980s. The main features of its approach included:

1. An extensive education programme in which every employee participated.

2. The eight most critical quality issues were identified and project groups set up to tackle them systematically and eradicate their root causes.

3. Recognition schemes and quality awards.

4. Continuous action system. This is a practice of constant review of processes to eliminate unnecessary activities and obstacles to meeting customer expectations.

5. Vendor accreditation. Requiring suppliers to meet exacting quality standards.

TQM at Milliken

Simon Caulkin[5] has given a useful account of the approach adopted by Milliken. The European subsidiary of the US textile corporation based at Wigan won the European Quality Award in 1993. The parent company won the US Baldrige award in 1989.

Milliken adopted the Total Quality approach in 1981. It was 'a solid 117-year-old company', manufacturing-led and deeply traditional. Initially the focus was on internal measures of quality but from 1985 there was a new focus on customer attitudes and expectations. By the late 1980s the company was selectively using a wide range of supporting processes and technologies, including statistical quality control, just-in-time inventory control, Deming's PDCA cycle (Plan-do-check-act), welding these and other techniques into a distinctive Milliken approach. To underscore this the company used its own managers rather than outside trainers to teach and interpret the new thinking.

Following a visit to Japan by 24 senior managers in 1991 it was decided to follow the example set by some of the companies they visited and extend the concept of quality to embrace the business as a whole – its strategy, financial planning and business development. Now it divides the Total Quality drive into seven parts – quality, cost, delivery, innovation, safety, morale, and environment – each of which is supported by continuing education and quality assurance.

Steps to empower the workforce have been an important feature of the Milliken approach. Shop-floor workers are empowered to stop the production line when they see quality problems. Participation in Milliken's suggestion scheme (Opportunities for Improvement) is running at 25 suggestions per person per year in Europe; 85 per cent are implemented.

Spending on education and training has trebled since 1983 and all managers receive a minimum of 40 classroom hours a year. Self-managed teams are being steadily phased in. Remuneration systems reward quality not quantity.

Many UK businesses could learn much from Milliken in the sphere of recognition. Throughout the company's plants notice boards prominently display performance-related charts, graphs and tables and achievements of the day, week and month. Recognition is seen as an essential element in the 'quality way of life'.

The Milliken story provides clear evidence that a Total Quality approach can work providing it is consistently pursued on a broad front over a number of years. Among the benefits Milliken derived were a 90 per cent reduction in costs arising from non conformance to specification; delivery performance up to 99.9 per cent; and an outstanding safety record. All contributed to outstanding business performance in terms of profitable growth.

Total Quality in Local Government – Brent Council

Brent Council's experience has been described in *Management Today* March 1994[6]. The 'trigger for change' for Brent Council was a financial crisis in 1988 resulting in 1000 job cuts out of a total payroll of 7000 and which left basic services in disarray. Since then the chief executive, Charles Wood, has been driving a programme of radical change in structure, systems and culture.

The Council first committed itself to becoming a customer-focused organization in 1990. In that year it carried out a customer satisfaction survey and an employee attitude survey. A vision statement was developed and a performance appraisal system introduced. In 1991 the Total Quality Programme was launched, proclaiming Brent's mission – to be the best local authority in the country. The core values were identified as Quality, Efficiency, and Putting the Customer First. A fourth, Valuing and Empowering Staff, was added later. A set of organizational beliefs was also identified:

O strong, committed leadership;

O the client/contractor split;

O Total Quality;

O clear accountability;

O customer-led services;

O total ownership;

O single, direct communication;

O maximum devolution;

O strong staff development.

The number of departments was reduced from 10 to five (housing, environmental services, social services, central services, education and arts and libraries) and the number of executive directors from 10 to five also. Of those, three were new to the organization. The number of senior managers was reduced by a third. Fixed-term contracts were introduced alongside performance-related pay.

A senior management development programme was held at the end of 1991, followed by training 300 quality facilitators and the introduction of 'quality time' – two hours each month during which staff give their ideas on how to improve service.

In May 1992 Wood held two mass meetings of Council employees at the Wembley Conference Centre to emphasize face-to-face the drive for quality.

Continuing processes include the installation of local computer networks, the institution of customer-focus groups, a new complaints procedure and over 70 customer surveys. Local taxation has been reduced by 46 per cent over a two-and-a-half year period and surveys show significant improvements in customer satisfaction.

Examples of the Council's new customer focus include a 'one-stop-shop' and a new Registry Office. The former is a carpeted area where courteous uniformed staff deal with enquiries and complaints. There are no queues, no overflowing ashtrays, no gloomy worn paintwork or other familiar features of the local government scene. There is a well-stocked children's play area and a vending machine. The Registry Office was moved into the Town Hall from dingy premises elsewhere and opens onto well-kept gardens. Couples are offered music or poetry readings of their choice at wedding ceremonies.

A basic structural change has involved separating the providers of services from those who commission them. This client/contractor split is supported by a considerable degree of devolvement of decision making. There are now 450 commissioning staff and 150 or so free-standing business units employing 4000 people. Some private sector and voluntary sector contractors are also involved but there is no specific privatization objective.

By the end of 1993 the feeling was growing that becoming Britain's best local authority was an attainable goal.

FACTORS MAKING FOR SUCCESS IN TQM

George Binney[7], reporting on an extensive survey of TQM initiatives, found that the most successful applications shared four characteristics:

1. *'Forthright' but listening leaders*. Leaders who were not prepared to compromise about quality standards and who made it quite clear that customer satisfaction was the number one priority. Nevertheless they were good at listening to employees' views and (equally important) acting on their ideas and suggestions.

2. *Provoking but not imposing change*. Getting people at all levels involved.

3. *Integrating quality into the heart of the business*. Getting people to see quality as everyone's responsibility, not some-

thing confined to a particular team, department or function. The concept of the 'internal customer' is important here. Pascale[8] talks about 'being quality' not just 'doing quality', referring to the need for emotional commitment and the adoption of a quality consciousness.

4. *Learning by doing*. Allowing time for experimentation and learning, encouraging feedback, letting people try out new ideas and take risks without fear of blame or ridicule.

BUSINESS PROCESS RE-ENGINEERING

Business Process Re-engineering (BPR) is an approach to radical or transformational change which focuses on questioning the need for and the means of carrying out each of the many processes involved in the organization's task. 'Processes' are defined in terms of activities which contribute to the delivering of the final product or service and the creation of a satisfied customer. Such activities frequently involve a flow across the organization, crossing functional and departmental boundaries. The aim is to re-design them so that customer's interests come first rather than what is most convenient for particular organizational sub-units.

Figure 6.2 shows a typical structure of an activity before BPR, and Figure 6.3 the same operation after restructuring.

Despite the use of the term 'engineering' the approach is in wide use by service and public sector organizations as well as ones in manufacturing.

Organizations which have experienced re-engineering report that adjustment to a process-based form of organization is more difficult for managers than for shop-floor employees. One obvious reason why this should be so is that BPR frequently leads to de-layering and consequent managerial redundancies. Another reason is that BPR breaks up long-established organizational 'empires'. Managers also find it difficult sometimes to think and act outside the boundaries of the function in which they have worked all their managerial careers thus far.

112

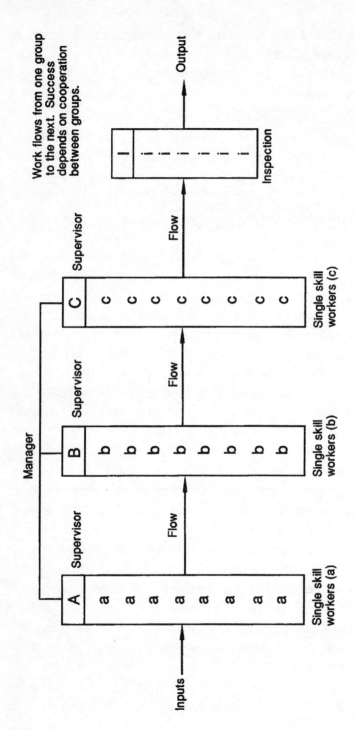

Figure 6.2 Typical structure before re-engineering

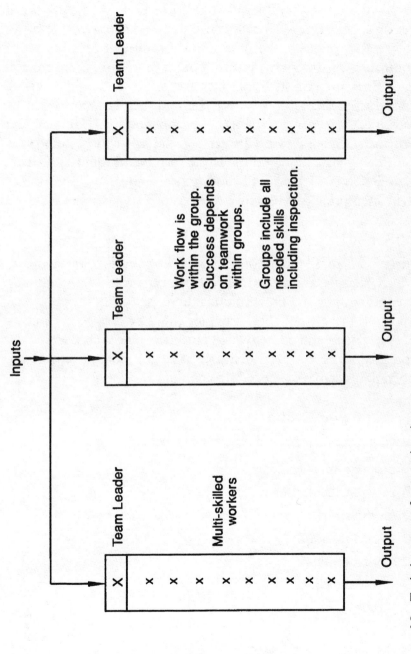

Figure 6.3 Typical structure after re-engineering

At the time of writing, BPR appears to be gaining ground as a favoured means of achieving transformation in organizational performance. Peter Bartram, writing in *Management Today* in July 1994[9], quotes a recent survey showing that 56 per cent of companies in Europe with turnovers of more than $250 million have BPR projects in hand, and that a further 22 per cent are considering the idea. Bartram distinguishes between what he calls the 'big bang' approach, exemplified by National and Provincial and BT (see Chapter 9), and what most companies aim for – what he describes as the 'patchwork quilt approach'. This involves picking individual processes for re-design rather than attempting to re-engineer the business as a whole.

BPR in ICL

In ICL a simple model of process re-engineering was adopted, which became known as the '30 per cent rule'. By examining everything they did organizational units or functions found that up to 30 per cent of their activities could be dropped; a further 30 per cent ought to be owned elsewhere since there was widespread duplication of effort; and a further 30 per cent of the operation's activities needed streamlining.

BPR in Rover Group

Rover Group has defined nine key business processes:

O product improvement;
O new product introduction;
O logistics;
O sales/distribution/service;
O manufacture;
O maintenance;
O business planning;
O corporate learning;
O management of people.

Strategic milestones have been identified, which are levels of achievement to be attained over a five year period. To set these, benchmarking was used to establish current best-in-class practice.

The key features of Rover's programme for process improvement are:

○ add value;

○ minimum interfaces;

○ suitable time horizons;

○ shorter cycles;

○ best-practice related;

○ stakeholder involvement (owners, customers, suppliers and employees).

BPR in Xerox

At Xerox the view was taken that the best way to implement real change was to understand the role of process, in particular the management process. In re-designing the management process at executive level the number of meetings per month for the executive team was cut from 17 to four.

The other key aspect of the process re-engineering was to make the processes cross-functional rather than just functional.

Xerox identified nine key business processes, just about every one of which was cross-functional.

Xerox distinguishes between business process simplification and re-engineering. The former can take about three months and effects improvements in cycle time and resource utilization without involving radical organizational change. It can produce improvements of up to 100 per cent in efficiency. The latter involves significant organization structure and information systems change, is unlikely to take less than nine months and results in improvements in efficiency up to 1000 per cent.

BPR at Xerox involves five main phases.

1. Develop the business vision and process objectives, prioritizing the objectives and setting challenging targets that are deemed impossible to achieve given existing processes and systems.
2. Identify the processes to be re-engineered, particularly ones critical for success or causing bottlenecks.
3. Understand and measure the existing processes.
4. Explore new approaches using IT.
5. Design, test and implement the new processes.

Bartram quotes David Harvey as having set out a number of success factors including the following:

○ Establish a clear view of strategic purpose.
○ Ensure top-management commitment.
○ Set challenging goals (world class standards of quality and productivity, for example).
○ Define the core processes.
○ Re-design the processes so as to create 'higher level' processes which form major end-to-end activities.
○ Manage the change process effectively.
○ Create ways of facilitating teamwork between staff from different functions.
○ Use effective project management techniques.
○ Adopt a 'stakeholder' approach.

BPR in Sun Life[11]

At the end of the 1980s, John Reeve, Sun Life's managing director, called for a radical business review. One of the findings was that the company's service levels were perceived by brokers as merely average. A thorough review of core processes followed, using consultants.

For example, issuing a new life assurance policy was a typical core process involving administrative steps carried out in different departments. No one was responsible for the whole process from beginning to end. At various stages there were errors or delays. A process which should have taken 15 days took 46.

In June 1991 Sun Life began re-engineering its core processes in a two-year, three-wave programme. Each process went through six stages: documentation of existing process; analysis; brainstorming ideas; evaluating solutions; detailed re-design; and implementation.

But tackling the processes was not enough. The company saw that for the changes to be wholly effective the new processes would need to be supported by fresh approaches to organization, people and technology. In particular there was a need to change from an organization based on functional specialists to one based on multi-skilled employees. The seven-layer management structure was replaced by one consisting of customer service managers and multi-disciplinary work teams with team leaders, with support from a trainer and a technical expert. New reward structures were introduced, based on pay for competencies and customer-related performance measures.

Results included improvements in process cycle times of between 40 and 90 per cent, a 10 per cent reduction in the unit cost of some processes and quality improvements (work performed right first time) of between 40 and 90 per cent.

BT

BT's experience with BPR began in 1987 with its attempt to develop a new computer system to support the process of supplying and repairing telephones. The plan ran into the difficulty that the different BT regions had their own methods and approaches. To cope with this BT created a 'Strategic Systems Plan' which tackled the issue of how the company might become a process-based organization. In 1990 the regional structure gave way to an organization based on market segments – business communications, personal communications, and special businesses (for example mobile communications).

In 1992 BT set up a new unit charged with defining the company's core and sub-processes and modelling how they ran across the new divisions. As explained by Roger Cartwright,

BT's business model manager[12], the processes were grouped under three headings:

○ *business processes* – which deliver products and services;

○ *support processes* – which help the business processes work, for example personnel and finance;

○ *component processes* – activities common to both business and support processes, such as billing.

In 1993 a further initiative, sponsored by Michael Hepher and labelled 'Breakout', was launched. The aim is to make more radical change possible by giving managers the power to change things outside the boundaries of their own divisions. According to Cartwright 'until the Breakout project, process management had been adopted half-heartedly by some of our top people.'

British Alcan Aluminium

This company is an example of the 'patchwork quilt' approach. The starting point was a need to improve efficiency and deliver better customer service. It learned much from its relationship with a sister company, Nippon Light Metal.

Each process re-engineering project has four stages – preparation, classroom training, analysis and design, and reorganization.

The preparation stage takes about a month and involves developing an understanding of the problem and explaining options.

The classroom training phase uses a computerized simulation exercise in which the trainee managers re-engineer an imaginary quotation process.

The analysis and design phase takes about five days during which the design team works with a facilitator. The implementation process follows and usually takes about a month.

As an example of a project, one British Alcan subsidiary was falling well behind schedule on a contract and 'the shop floor was piled high with inventory'. The BPR team altered plant layout, made small design changes to the product, introduced multi-skilled work teams, eliminated redundant stock and introduced a just-in-time scheduling system. Within three months the company was ahead of schedule with virtually 100 per cent on-time delivery. Equally important, the contract was renewed.

Describing the company's experience, Ian Woolven, business analyst[13], points out that the 'patchwork quilt' approach has produced real benefits, but that these are 'isolated islands of re-engineered processes'. He goes on to accept that 'We can't put our hands on our hearts and say that we have produced a miracle transformation of our whole business.'

The Benefits of BPR

Without doubt the most authoritative and comprehensive study of UK companies' experience of BPR to date is the Business Intelligence report *Re-engineering: The Critical Success Factors*[14]. This gives considerable detailed information on applications in such organizations as Baxi Partnership, BT, Cigna Employee Benefits, Lucas Industries automotive division, Pilkington Optronics, Reuters, and Western Provident. The benefits included the following:

○ Significant increase in productivity (Baxi).
○ Reduction from 17 days to two in the time taken to issue a quote (Cigna).
○ Manufacturing lead times down from 55 days to 12 and order to despatch times from 105 days to 32 (Lucas).
○ Manufacturing lead times cut from 15 to seven months (Pilkington Optronics).
○ Time taken to process new medical insurance business down from 28 days to four (Western Provident).

THE 'SOFT' ISSUES

According to Eddie Obeng[15] the early examples of re-engineering programmes led to failure in many instances because of concentration on tackling the 'hard' issues such as processes and systems. The very term 'business process' suggests that this is what it is all about. Yet, in his view, the 'soft' issues involved –

the reactions of people, the changes needed in people's behaviour, the impact on the skill requirements and the changes in culture and values – are at least as critical, often more so. He gives an account of re-engineering programmes in two financial services companies which set out to change their cultures before embarking on full-blown BPR.

The first company, Cigna UK, found that its first attempts to introduce BPR were hampered by failure to involve the staff and to give adequate attention to cultural factors. They started over again with regular meetings to explain what re-engineering and teamwork involved and what would be expected of people in the new environment. The eventual outcome of the programme was to transform six separate functions into two processes – pre-sale and post-sale activities. The time taken to give a quotation was reduced from 17 to two days and staff who previously handled 30 to 40 claims a day could now deal with between 75 and 90. Costs were significantly reduced and an underwriting loss of £2 million eliminated.

A key element in the success achieved at Cigna was the approach of allowing teams of relatively junior staff to develop their own processes. 'It brought people from administration, claims and accounts and simply moved them around a single desk.' This approach has the clear advantage that having created the new processes themselves the teams are much more likely to feel a sense of ownership. 'In effect the creation of the process works as an important means of cultural change.'

In the second case described by Obeng – the National & Provincial Building Society – there was a firm intention to start by changing the culture. A top-down approach was followed, instigated by a new top management team and beginning with a week of meetings involving the top ten executives which led to a new mission statement focusing on customer needs. The board was re-styled 'the direction management team' and heads of functions and business divisions were re-titled as directors of customer engagement or customer requirements. The new approach was then communicated to 150 of the company's senior managers. The company aims to reduce eight levels of management and 20 grades to three and four respectively. It is introducing competency-based assessment and performance-related pay. There are plans to install a new IT system at a cost in the region of £20 million.

With this approach goes a clear message – management is not immune to change – the sacrifices begin at the top.

References

1. Crosby, Philip (1984) *Quality Without Tears,* McGraw Hill, New York.

2. Matthyssens, P and Van den Bulte, C 'Getting closer and getting nicer: partnerships in the supply chain', *Long Range Planning* Vol 27 No 1 February 1994.

3. Walker, Robb 'Rank Xerox' – management revolution', *Long Range Planning* Vol 25 No 1 February 1992.

4. Bower, David 'Becoming a learning organization – the experience of the Rover Group' in Philip Sadler (ed) (1993), *Learning More About Learning Organizations,* AMED, London.

5. Caulkin, Simon 'The road to peerless Wigan', *Management Today,* March 1994.

6. van de Vliet, Anita 'The Brent Conversion', *Management Today,* March 1994.

7. Binney, George 'Rising above the bureaucracy of quality', *Directions: The Ashridge Journal,* May 1993.

8. Pascale, Richard T (1991) *Managing on the Edge,* Penguin Books, London.

9. Bartram, Peter 'Re-engineering revisited', *Management Today,* July 1994.

10. Walker, Robb, *op. cit.*

11. Oliver, Judith 'Shocking to the core', *Management Today,* August 1993.

12. Cartwright, Roger 'British Telecom sprints on the spot', *Management Today,* July 1994.

13. Woolven, Jan 'British Alcan Aluminium paces itself', *Management Today,* July 1994.

14. Business Intelligence Report (1994) *Re-engineering: the Critical Success Factors,* Business Intelligence Ltd, London.

15. Obeng, Eddie (1994) *Making Re-engineering Happen,* FT/Pitman, London.

7

The Learning Organization – Change as a Way of Life

Ultimately, organizational vitality and adaptiveness depend on learning.
                                                                Pascale

Of the many definitions of the learning organization perhaps the most apt is that of Pedler, Boydell and Burgoyne[1], 'An organization which facilitates the learning of all its members and continually transforms itself'.

To describe a company as a 'learning organization' implies that the activities of the organization as a whole are more or less continually monitored to provide feedback which is then used as a basis for learning how to improve performance. The concept is applicable to discrete events involving a single actor (for example conducting an employment interview) at one extreme, through more complex processes involving many actors (launching a new product), to the achievement of strategic objectives by the organization as a whole.

It represents an approach to the development of managerial performance which must be recognized as an ideal – constantly to be striven for, but in practice extremely difficult to achieve.

The reasons for this reflect the complexity of organizational life and in particular:

○ the timescale over which feedback takes place is such that the situation has changed by the time the learning has occurred;

○ the actors themselves change;

○ knowledge of results is always less than perfect, and often highly subjective;

O the same event or process does not recur in identical or closely similar form.

Barriers to the learning process are often formidable. For example, feedback fails to flow undistorted through the filters of power, status and authority. Success leads to complacency – 'we have nothing to learn'. Failure leads to a witch hunt – 'who was to blame?'. Nevertheless, the ideal remains worth striving for, and can be seen as an important element in an organization's system of values.

ORGANIZATIONAL VERSUS INDIVIDUAL LEARNING

It is important to be quite clear about the nature of the learning process, and the level at which it takes place. In the last analysis learning can only take place at the level of the individual. Individuals can, of course, learn how to do things by themselves (individual behaviour), how to do things as members of groups (team behaviour), and how to do things as members of organizations (organization behaviour). As a result of such learning processes on the part of individuals, groups and organizations perform more effectively, and in this sense we can speak of group or organizational learning.

There is, however, a further organizational effect – the transfer of learning within the organization – which can be either direct and immediate or indirect and deferred. Direct and immediate transfer takes place by means such as in-company training courses, counselling, appraisal and coaching. Indirect and deferred transfer takes place in a variety of ways through which an organization stores its accumulated learning, ranging from systems and procedures for dealing with recurring situations to policy statements, management manuals and deliberate or spontaneous culture change. Induction training is very much concerned with the transfer of this type of learning to new members of the organization. Hedberg[2] argues that 'although organizational learning occurs through individuals it would be a mistake to conclude that organization learning is nothing bar the cumulative result of their members' learning. Organizations do not have brains but they have cognitive systems and memories.'

The complex processes and influences involved in organizational learning are illustrated in Figure 7.1.

LEARNING AND INNOVATION

The model developed thus far lends itself well to the situation in which learning takes place on the basis of feedback from experience in a continuous way. This works when the experience is itself continuous, but the model runs into difficulty when there is discontinuity of experience and an organization has to learn fast how to cope with a novel problem or situation not encompassed by its previous experience.

Examples include:

O first time experience of exporting;

O carrying out a major acquisition;

O meeting a new source of competition.

The first requirement is to perceive the novel situation as one giving rise to a need to learn. The second is to select appropriate vehicles for learning.

There are some obvious examples, such as the organization may not have met the problem before, but some members may have done so in the course of previous experience with other employers. (Managerial mobility is thus an important means of organizational learning which some organizations deny themselves.) Consultants can, of course, be brought in, but much depends on the role they play. An organization which functions as a learning system uses consultants as a resource from which to learn how to solve a problem. An organization which gives the problem to the consultants to solve will learn little from the process.

Specially designed training programmes can be set up internally or externally with the objective of achieving rapid learning

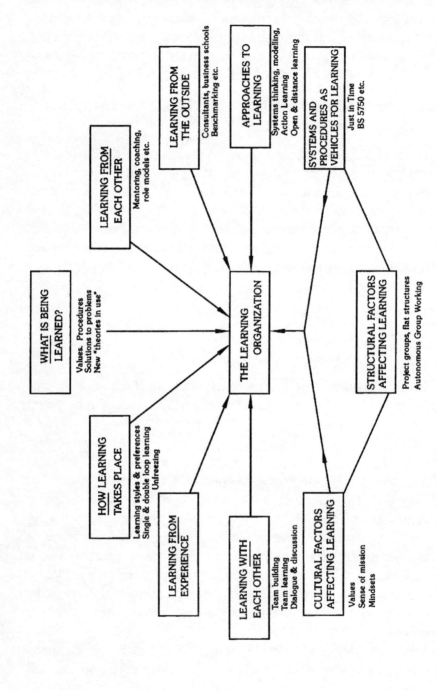

Figure 7.1 Learning organizations – the processes and the influences

in the particular area in which the problem lies. Some recent examples of this kind in the UK include managing a contracting rather than expanding organization, or learning to work with a matrix organization.

'UNLEARNING' IN ORGANIZATIONS

'Unlearning' is more difficult to achieve than learning. It involves the ability to identify patterns of thinking and acting which were appropriate and relevant in the past but have ceased to be useful or have even become counter-productive, to 'unfreeze' them and to substitute new and more appropriate ones. There is abundant evidence from case studies and other sources that this rarely happens and that organizations persist in habitual behaviour long after it has ceased to be appropriate. Examples from UK industry include carrying high levels of inventory or persevering with very hierarchical management structures.

Almost certainly the organization will need outside help in the form of a change agent of some kind to assist both the diagnosis and the implementation of change.

THE FIFTH DISCIPLINE

The most comprehensive treatment of the concept of the learning organization in a single volume remains Peter Senge's *The Fifth Discipline*[3].

He begins by quoting Arie de Geus, head of planning for Royal Dutch/Shell:

> The ability to learn faster than your competitors may be the only sustainable competitive advantage.

He goes on to assert that the organizations which will succeed in future will be those which find out how to make use of people's capacity to learn at *all* levels.

Learning organizations are possible, he argues, because it is in our nature to learn and because 'we love to learn'. Also people are searching for meaning and fulfilment in their work.

Senge points to a growing number of business leaders who feel part of a profound revolution in the nature of work. But the most important reason for building learning organizations in his view is that we are only now beginning to understand the capabilities that such organizations need to possess – the basic disciplines that they will need to master. Senge identifies five such 'disciplines':

1. *Personal mastery* – a special level of proficiency achieved through commitment to life-long learning.
2. *Mental models* – learning how to surface, challenge and adapt our mental models, our strongly held assumptions and generalizations that determine our understanding of the world around us.
3. *Building a shared vision* – where there is a genuine vision people become capable of outstanding achievements and significant learning takes place because of strong motivations.
4. *Team learning* – teams can learn and when this happens they excel while at the same time their members are developing. Team learning is essential since teams and not individuals are the 'fundamental learning unit in modern organizations'.
5. *Systems thinking* – the ability to think in terms of the whole rather than the component parts.

Systems thinking is the fifth discipline since it is the one that integrates all the disciplines. But systems thinking needs the other disciplines if it is to realize its potential.

Senge reminds us that few organizations live even half as long as a person. For example, of the *Fortune* 500 firms in 1970, one third had disappeared from the list by 1983. This, he argues, is the result of poor learning. The way organizations have traditionally been designed has created 'learning disabilities'. These are seven in number:

1. *'I am my position'* – people identify themselves with particular functions or tasks rather than with the overall purpose.
2. *'The enemy is out there'* – finding someone else or something else to blame when things go wrong.
3. *The illusion of taking charge* – being reactive instead of truly proactive.
4. *Fixation on events and short-term results* – instead of on slower gradual processes.
5. *The parable of the boiled frog* – if a frog is placed in a pan of boiling water it will jump out. Place it in a pan of water at room temperature and raise the temperature slowly, and the frog will sit there until it boils.
6. *The delusion of learning from experience* – when our actions have consequences which are spread over years it becomes impossible to learn from experience.
7. *The myth of the management team* – having the appearance rather than the reality of a cohesive management team.

THE CHARACTERISTICS OF A LEARNING ORGANIZATION

The characteristics of a learning organization have been set out by Andrew Mayo[4] and can be summarized as follows:

1. The word 'learning' is frequently heard and is part of the every day language.
2. Managers see development of the people they are responsible for as a key element in the job.
3. Documents used in appraisal and development planning make provision for learning plans to be mutually devised by the individual and his/her manager.
4. Giving and receiving feedback is normal practice and people are trained in the process.
5. Managers and others can diagnose their preferred learning styles and go on to select from a variety of learning methods.

6. Individuals are proactive in developing their own learning and supportive of colleagues in theirs.

7. People are interested in analyzing incidents and events so as to learn from them. They constantly question the way things are done in the search for improvement.

8. Looking for someone or something to blame when things go wrong is unacceptable behaviour. The emphasis is upon 'what can we learn from this?'.

9. People focus on the learning opportunities offered by jobs rather than on the status that goes with them.

10. The 'not invented here' attitude is rejected. Ideas and experience are shared *across* teams.

11. The organization has an accessible, user-friendly, updated database.

12. The organization continually benchmarks itself against 'best practice'.

13. Spontaneous and informal networks exist and are seen as legitimate.

There are certain conditions which need to be present if the learning organization is to become a reality.

These include:

1. Role-modelling by top management, by being seen both to be learning themselves and as involved with the learning of others.

2. Effective horizontal and diagonal as well as vertical communication channels.

3. Rewards which reinforce the motivation to learn.

4. Effective systems for scanning the environment.

5. Active involvement in joint ventures, strategic alliances, etc.

6. A culture fostering openness, sharing of information, and egalitarianism. (Pascale refers to the 'integrity of contention management processes – the surfacing of hard truths and confronting reality.')

7. Employees are empowered to apply their learning to the way they do their jobs.

The factors which inhibit organizational learning include:

1. Fixation on short-term results and exclusively on 'bottom-line' indicators of performance.
2. The assumption that experience by itself automatically leads to learning.
3. A long history of success (as in the case of IBM).

DOUBLE-LOOP LEARNING

Chris Argyris[5] has pointed out that learning takes place at more than one level. The first level, which he calls single-loop learning, is exemplified by the thermostat which, when it detects a deviation from the temperature it is set at, takes corrective action. If the thermostat was able to question whether the temperature it was set at was the appropriate one for the circumstances it would be involved in double-loop learning. Double-loop learning, then, involves questioning fundamental beliefs and assumptions. Single-loop learning is fine for routine matters and for when things are stable. More complex issues such as strategy and conditions of rapid change call for double-loop learning.

Argyris also draws a distinction between *espoused* theories – people's stated beliefs and assumptions – and *theories-in-use* – the beliefs and assumptions people actually draw upon when acting. He argues that the theory-in-use which most managers have learnt through the process of socialization is based on the need to feel in control, to win out in conflict situations and to save face. Managers with such a theory-in-use will inhibit organizational learning by creating conditions of undiscussability, self-fulfilling prophecies, self-sealing processes and escalating error.

If double-loop learning is to take place individuals must be able to alter their theory-in-use and to become much more open, less defensive, more willing to listen, and so on. Argyris optimistically believes most people would prefer to behave in this way, given a favourable climate. He suggests the following steps as a means of helping organizations learn at the double-loop level.

1. Help individuals become aware of their theories-in-use.
2. Invite top management to write cases on issues of current importance and to meet and discuss them. They then begin to see how issues become undiscussable.
3. Help people develop a new theory-in-use.
4. These people then introduce new actions into their organization and help others to learn them.
5. As top managers and others begin to develop new actions they will also develop new learning systems which in turn will lead to new reward systems and control and evaluation procedures.

Argyris' ideal theory-in-use, which in his view would enhance double-loop learning, is based on the valuing of valid data, free and informed choice, internal commitment to the choice, and constant monitoring of its implementation. The related behaviours include sharing control with those who have competence, combining advocacy with enquiry, illustrating attributions and evaluations with directly observable data, surfacing conflict, and testing hypotheses publicly.

Rover Learning Company

Rover identified 'corporate learning' as one of nine key business processes, defining it as the process by which the business identifies, acquires, disseminates, retains, shares, and updates useful knowledge.

David Bower[6] has described how, in order to develop and improve this process, it set up the Rover Learning Company. This is a business within the business, with its own chairman, managing director, executive committee and board of governors. Its aim is to provide a first class service in learning and development opportunities for all employees. Its first chairman was Sir

Graham Day, chairman at the time of the Rover Group. His appointment raised the profile of learning and development within the company.

A corporate learning database was set up. This is computer-based and provides for the capture of key learning points across all aspects of the business. It can be accessed by all employees.

Rover Learning Business's first initiative, however, in May 1990, was the REAL programme (Rover Employees Assisted Learning). This scheme entitled any employee to receive up to £100 a year for pursuing virtually any kind of learning programme.

Unipart U

Unipart U is the company 'university' of Unipart. Opened in 1993 its mission is 'to train and inspire people to achieve world-class standards of performance within the Unipart Group and among its stakeholders.' John Neil, describing its purpose to delegates at the 1994 annual convention of the Institute of Directors, said that the top team at Unipart took the view that learning and training were not separate activities carried out by consultants or outside agents but were 'fundamentally and inextricably linked with the very being of our company'.

A 'dean's group' was created, comprising divisional managing directors with their own faculties responsible for ensuring that high quality training courses are available to their employees. Each of the deans has written and has presented training courses in the 'U', where managers and employees at all levels will teach each other.

The part-time principal of the 'university' is Professor Dan Jones, co-author of *The Machine That Changed the World*.

LEARNING AND ORGANIZATIONAL EFFECTIVENESS

In their comprehensive study of the concept of the learning organization, Andrew Mayo and Elizabeth Lank[7] face up to the need to demonstrate the impact of organizational learning on business results. They point out that improved performance may not come about quickly and remind us that few investments pay off in the first year or so. They also make the point that some costs and lost revenues are invisible, for example it is impossible to assess the value of any contracts lost or the number of new customers the organization has failed to attract because of slow and inadequate learning about what is happening in the market place.

They argue the case for regarding people and their skills and knowledge as assets of the corporation just as much as cash, plant and equipment, and buildings. Learning increases the level of knowledge and skill and so enhances the value of these assets. This incremental value, however, does not as yet feature on the balance sheet, despite the fact that other 'intangibles' such as goodwill, the value of a brand and of intellectual property do get taken into account.

Mayo and Lank recommend four courses of action for organizations so as to ensure that the financial implications of learning are given proper attention.

1. Study the 'hidden costs' and 'lost revenues' that are the result of failures to learn.

2. Measure the added value created by teams and individuals and show how this is increased by learning.

3. Improve induction procedures so as to transfer knowledge and experience to new recruits.

4. Compare the costs and benefits of formal learning processes with other options.

References

1. Pedler, Mike, Boydell, Tom and Burgoyne, John 'Towards the learning company', *Management Education and Development* Vol 20 No 1 1989.

2. Hedberg, Bo 'How organizations learn and unlearn', in PC Nystrom and WH Starbuck (eds) (1981) *Handbook of Organization Design,* Vol 1, Oxford University Press.

3. Senge, Peter (1990) *The Fifth Discipline: The Art and Practice of the Learning Organization,* Doubleday, New York.

4. Mayo, Andrew 'Learning at all organizational levels', in Philip Sadler (ed) (1993) *Learning More About Learning Organizations,* AMED, London.

5. Argyris, Chris (1993) *On Organizational Learning,* Blackwell Business, Cambridge Mass.

6. Bower, David 'Becoming a learning organization – the experience of the Rover Group', in Philip Sadler *op. cit.*

7. Mayo, Andrew and Lank, Elizabeth (1994) *The Power of Learning. A Guide to Gaining Competitive Advantage,* Institute of Personnel Development, London.

8

Making it Happen – The Process of Implementation

HOW TO START?

There are two extreme approaches to launching a major programme of organizational change; to do so with as loud a bang as possible, or to begin softly. The first approach is typified by what happened in Unipart in 1987 when the change programme was launched by means of a four-hour theatrical show for all employees, complete with theme song.

The softly, softly approach is exemplified by cases where the starting point is a pilot experiment of some kind in one particular location, as in the case of Ford in America where pioneering work with developing the Employee Involvement (EI) programme, subsequently adopted company-wide, was carried out at Ford's Diversified Products Operations subsidiary. Much depends on the culture of the company, the leadership style of the chief executive, and the extent to which the ground has been prepared in advance so that a climate receptive to change already exists.

WHERE TO START?

As I explained in Chapter 2, organizations exist as systems, the principal components of which are structure, processes, and culture. It follows that organizational change, if it is to be effective, must be holistic, involving all the components so that change in one aspect reinforces change in others. The ideal approach, therefore, is to move forward simultaneously on all fronts. In practice, however, this is extremely difficult, partly due to the load thus placed on resources, particularly management time, but also because in almost every instance the ongoing activities of the organization have to be maintained during the period in which the change programme is carried out. Operational requirements will dictate the timing of some of the changes rather than what is ideal from the viewpoint of change management.

Given that changing the culture is almost certainly going to take a lot longer than altering the structure or introducing new processes, there is a valid case for beginning with actions designed to change the culture. Culture is to do with a widely shared set of values, characteristic behaviours and what some writers such as Pascale[1] refer to as the organization's *paradigm* and others such as Johnson[2] as the common *mindset*. This is a set of assumptions or beliefs which are taken for granted, rarely surfaced or discussed, which largely determine how people perceive the world.

Mindsets make people blind to possibilities and opportunities. They close down people's thinking and capacity for vision. One example of a mindset is how most of us unconsciously assume, when certain roles in our society are mentioned – the judge in a trial, the company chairman, the official receiver, the brain surgeon, the mining engineer – the person being referred to is male, while when certain other roles are mentioned – nurse or secretary, for example – we tend to assume the person is female.

In cases where companies have paved the way for change by developing a new mission statement a start will have been made in changing people's shared values, but this needs to be reinforced by actions aimed at bringing about change in characteristic behaviours and in the paradigm or mindset. The most powerful weapon for bringing such changes about is undoubtedly a particular form of training which is focused on changing attitudes, beliefs and behaviours rather than on imparting knowledge or skill. Such programmes of training, starting at the top and cascading down through the organization to shop-floor level, featured strongly in the early stages of the change programmes at British Airways, ICL and Rover.

The programme of organizational change which resulted in the remarkable transformation in performance at British Airways was largely driven by massive investment in training at every level, starting with top management. Of the top 150 people in BA – the policy makers and those with company-wide concerns – 30 at a time attended a one-week course known as Leading the Service Business 1.

BA directors were among the faculty and the content focused on critical business issues, drawing upon data from staff, customer and competitor research, and feedback of participants' profiles on a well-known personality test, the Myers Briggs Type Indicator.

At the next level down there were two three-day residential courses, spaced six weeks apart, for the management teams reporting to the top 150. This programme – Leading the Service Business 2 – focused on such issues as:

O Who are our external/internal customers and stakeholders and what do they expect of us?

O How does our performance compare with our 'functional competitors' in other companies?

O How can we contribute to profitability?

O How can we exploit IT?

O How do we work together as a team?

O Do we have the support and commitment of our staff?

Again, the faculty included directors of the corporation, including the chief executive and the finance director.

The outcome of each course included a clear mission for each team and plans for securing the involvement of staff in achieving it.

For all employees there was a one-day course entitled To Be the Best. This focused on customer expectations, customer-service standards, the competition, the achievement of inter-departmental team-work and the challenge of seeking continuous improvement.

The course was presented and facilitated by members of BA's middle management and included an opportunity for a dialogue with members of top management. The 'outputs' included suggestions for service improvements, a new focus on customers and competitors, and a greater understanding of the interdependence of the various parts of the organization. The opportunity was also taken to invite staff to express their concerns and to be reassured about the impact of change.

THE CONTRIBUTION OF THE HUMAN RESOURCE FUNCTION

Elmer Burack[3] argues that Human Resource Development (HRD) has a crucial role to play in successfully orchestrating strategic culture change. Don Beattie and FMK Tampoe[4] provide a detailed case of the role of HR in the change process at ICL.

The success of ICL's strategic change has been attributed to three main factors:

1. *Investment in people.* The 1992 ICL Corporate Review states 'our contribution to our customers' success depends first and foremost on the calibre of our people. It is why we spend heavily – £20 million in 1992 – on staff training and the systematic development of our employees' potential.'

2. *Flexibility and adaptability.* The shift from low volume, high margin, mainframe products to higher volume business involving a mix of hardware, software and service delivery called for considerable adaptability. Remaining responsive to customer needs calls for a high level of flexibility. Achieving this involves a major cultural shift towards a more entrepreneurial risk-taking culture.

3. *Quality*. ICL was one of the first UK companies to go for Total Quality Management (TQM). A continuous improvement process called Delta was also introduced, with the aim of 'improving a thousand things by 1 per cent rather than one thing by 1000 per cent'.

The Impact of the HR Function

ICL undertook a major review of its personnel function to provide a model of how it should develop in the light of changing business needs. Interviews were held with members of the ICL board and with senior, middle and junior managers. The results showed a need for several changes in emphasis. The personnel function as it was then was seen as too bureaucratic, creating too much paperwork, with over-cumbersome processes and confused accountability. Line managers wanted greater say in decisions about people but did not want to assume responsibility for the administrative work involved. Personnel specialists saw the need to improve and streamline administration and to become involved in managing change.

From this process a set of agreed objectives for the personnel function was developed, including the following:

○ to support the achievement of business goals;
○ to translate business plans into integrated human resource plans;
○ to be creative and assertive in the management of change;
○ to ensure the organization operates in a 'legal, honest and decent way'.

Additionally five distinct roles were identified:

○ leading edge expert on specialist subjects;
○ experienced specialist HR adviser;
○ business team contribution;
○ developing generalist – providing a general personnel service;

○ administrator server – maintaining efficient personnel systems and procedures.

ICL has a business review process which takes place three times a year. Part of this looks at people and organization development and involves line managers presenting to their colleagues issues to do with organization structure, skill requirements and training needs as well as identifying high potential individuals. The personnel function carries out similar reviews for its own staff every six months.

Personnel has developed a series of developmental seminars for personnel specialists including:

○ understanding the business;
○ the personnel function and its role;
○ resourcing;
○ organization design.

The function has also defined performance standards for personnel work including both 'hard' and 'soft' criteria.

For example, under the heading Organization Development, the standards are:

○ The organization structure is designed to support company and local strategies and give the necessary focus.
○ Departments have a clear statement of accountabilities for results which do not overlap.
○ Where matrix structures exist the network of functional relationships is understood and accountabilities are clear.
○ Opinion surveys are carried out and lead to an action plan at least once a year in each area.
○ Organization change is professionally managed with a documented communication plan, full statements outlining the change and questions/answers where appropriate.
○ Organization charts are always available and are updated quarterly.

○ Team building events are used to provide commitment to change.

Rover Group

In Rover Group the HR function also played a key role in transforming the company[5]. As part of the process it developed its own functional vision and mission statement.

ROVER'S PERSONNEL FUNCTION'S VISION

Success Through People – all associates willingly give their best contribution to achieve extraordinary customer satisfaction.

The Mission

To develop and facilitate the implementation of people strategies and plans to enable the Company to achieve its objectives.

Critical Success Factors

We must:
1. Create the culture which provides purpose, dignity and recognition to every individual in an environment of trust which is open, safe and secure.
2. Help the leaders lead by empowering and supporting them in pursuit of company goals.
3. Achieve world class resourcing standards, ensuring we have the right people in the right numbers with the right skills, in the right place or the right time – right first time.
4. Create continuous learning with development opportunities for everyone and sharing of best practice.
5. Ensure company-wide understanding of the compelling business needs by maintaining continuous dialogue.

---

6. Empower individuals and teams to achieve success through commitment, motivation, flexibility and skills development.

7. Foster positive involvement relationships with the broader Rover community.

Bosch

In the UK subsidiary of Bosch[6] TQM was adopted and the HR function was heavily involved through setting examples and bringing about culture change, defining corporate culture, supporting team-working, and so on.

The notion of the internal customer applies here. In HR the whole of the organization is the customer, and has the right to specify the service it expects and to comment on delivery. In Bosch HR they developed a customer service index. Total quality gives the HR function the opportunity to play a central role in the affairs of the organization. Measurement plays a key role. In HR the easy ones are absenteeism and labour turnover, the difficult areas are recruitment-cycle time, return on training investment, and employee attitudes.

THE USE OF SYMBOLISM

Cultural change involves leaving behind the traditional practices of the past and the organization's conventional wisdom. There are many ways in which the break with the past can be expressed powerfully using symbolism.

John Harvey-Jones[7] tells how, on becoming chairman of ICI, he moved board meetings from the imposing boardroom to his own office. The boardroom had been designed in an earlier era so as to emphasize the power of the chairman. Harvey-Jones, however, wanted the ICI board to operate more as a 'band of brothers' with free and uninhibited discussion and with people able to get up, walk around, pour themselves a cup of coffee, draw on flip charts and generally feel relaxed and unrestricted. Under the new arrangement the board members, instead of facing each other across a huge and impressive board-table, sat in conference chairs with small, adjustable side tables to take their papers. They sat, more often than not, in shirt sleeves and there were no fixed places. In this way the new chairman symbolized a radical change in management style.

Symbolism of a different kind was used in the transformation of British Airways by the adoption of a new livery. At the time the cost of repainting the whole of the BA fleet gave rise to considerable criticism. With hindsight, however, this symbolic act clearly had its place in a comprehensive programme of change, the pay-off from which more than justified the various investments made en route.

The importance of symbolism lies in the way it provides a clear message of a break with the past. Such actions as moving to open plan offices, abolishing reserved parking places, moving to single status catering arrangements or abolishing such traditional job titles as foreman or supervisor, can have a disproportionate impact on creating a climate receptive to change.

ANTICIPATING AND WORKING THROUGH RESISTANCE TO CHANGE

Resistance to change is almost always unavoidable, but its strength can be minimized by careful advance planning which involves thinking through the factors in the check-list below:

O Who will be affected by the proposed changes?

   — directly affected;

   — indirectly affected.

O From *their* point of view, what aspects of their working lives will be affected?

reporting relationships	earnings
relations with co-workers	pension
employment security	job satisfaction
training needs	other benefits

career prospects   status

skill requirements   workload

working conditions   journey to work

working hours

○ *Who* should communicate information about change, *when* and by what *means*?

○ What management style is to be used?

— *Autocratic* – change imposed from above.

— *Persuasive* – attempt to persuade people of the need to go along with changes which top management believes to be necessary.

— *Consultative* – consult employees (through their representatives or directly via an opinion survey) and present a programme of change based on this process of consultation.

— *Fully participative* – only proceed with a programme of change provided a substantial majority of employees is in favour.

THE KEY ROLE OF LEADERSHIP

Kotter and Heskett[8] describe 10 cases of organizational transformation in the US, Europe and Japan, including such well known cases as British Airways and ICI in Britain, GE and Xerox in America, SAS in Scandinavia, and Nissan in Japan. In all 10 the transformation followed the appointment of an individual with a track record of outstanding leadership. Colin Marshall, John Harvey-Jones, Jack Welch, David Kearns, Jan Carlzon and Yutaka Kume are the role models for chief executives seeking to lead transformational change in their own organizations.

Mansour Javidan[9] has identified six key roles which such leaders play:

1. *Being a visionary* – having a deep understanding of where the organization is currently and how it got there and devel-

oping a clear sense of future direction. The vision is developed through a process of consultation which helps ensure commitment.

2. *Acting as a symbolizer* – successful leaders practice what they preach, they lead by example and are willing to place the organization's interests above their own. They are able to articulate the vision.

3. *The leader as innovator* – being willing to do new things and accept new ideas but also able to create an atmosphere in which others feel encouraged to be innovative.

4. *The auditor role* – monitoring and assessing the organization's performance against high performance standard.

5. *The ambassador* – representing the organization to the outside world.

6. *The mobilizer* – turning the vision into reality involves drawing to the fullest possible extent on the abilities and energy of the workforce. This in turn involves empowering people, which means removing any aspects of the working environment which present people from doing their best work.

He goes on to set out what he sees as the critical attributes of successful leaders.

1. A strong self-image – high self-confidence and trust in one's own judgement.

2. A strong drive – ambitious both for themselves and for their organizations.

3. Functional competence which is a key factor in their credibility.

4. A deep knowledge of the organization.

5. High energy level.

6. Strong belief in their subordinates.

7. Concerned about their subordinates – caring.

Leader Commitment

If top management is to be effective in leading transformational change its members must display, in both word and deed, a very high level of commitment to the organization and to its goals, together with a high level of concern for employees. This commitment will show itself in a number of ways, including:

○ the ability to articulate a vision of what the organization could become in such a way that the speaker's passionate commitment comes across;

○ sticking with the organization rather than pursuing potentially more fruitful career prospects elsewhere;

○ consistently putting the interests of the organization as a whole above sectional or divisional interests;

○ a high personal work-rate;

○ involvement in training and development.

Negative indicators will include:

○ high salary or bonus increases at times when other employees are experiencing hardship;

○ preoccupation with protecting and bolstering own image and status;

○ consistent use of evidently borrowed buzz-words and rhetoric;

○ not being an employee – as was so until recently in the case of the BBC's director general, John Birt.

The Leader's Concern for Employees

This implies a sincere and genuinely held perception of the organization as 'all one team'.

Positive indicators that this is the case include:

○ use of compulsory redundancy only as a last resort and, if resorted to, on generous terms and providing those affected with a wide-range of support services;

○ above-average levels of investment in training and development;

○ single-status personnel policies and conditions of employment;

○ showing trust in employees (for example no clocking on and
off);

○ management by walking about;

○ standard company dress.

Negative indicators include:

○ pulling rank to obtain privileges;

○ adopting attitudes of superiority and demanding deferential
behaviour;

○ separate dining arrangements;

○ withholding information.

THE IMPORTANCE OF INVOLVEMENT

Involvement implies that both the problem and the proposed
solution are 'owned' by the people concerned. When people are
involved they see the problem which triggers a need for change
as *their* problem, not someone else's such as 'the management'.
But for the change process to be successful they also need to feel
ownership of the solution to the problem, ie the proposed
changes.

The best way to ensure ownership of the problem is to make
clear to the people concerned how it affects them, their jobs,
their futures. The best way to ensure ownership of the solution is
to invite people to share in the process of developing it.
Generating ownership of problem and solution in this way is not
too difficult in cases involving no redundancies, or at least no
compulsory redundancies, but becomes extremely difficult if not
impossible if compulsory redundancy in significant numbers is
part of the proposed changes.

The process of working through potential resistance to change among employees at Ind Coope's Burton Brewery has been described by Cox[10]. The change programme began in October 1983 and continued for five years. The starting point was a video presentation which made the following points:

○ The company's future survival was at stake.

○ The jobs which the business was capable of sustaining needed protecting – but this was a smaller number of jobs than presently existed.

○ Given acceptance of the need for flexibility, redeployment and/or retraining there would be no compulsory redundancy.

○ There was a desire to involve people more in the running of the business.

○ There was a need to sort out outdated procedures and agreements that had led to friction and conflict in the past.

This video was shown to all employees in groups of 150 within the space of one week. These presentations were introduced by the chief executive. All the questions asked on these occasions and all the answers were recorded, published and distributed to all employees within seven days. The first six months of the change process was then taken up with consultation with employees. The core philosophy for implementing change was to spread ownership and involve as many people as possible. Team-working was used as the means of involving as many people as possible in helping to finalize the design of the changes.

UNDERSTANDING THE POLITICS OF ORGANIZATIONAL CHANGE

The legitimate power of the board of directors, appointed by the shareholders, is not the sole power base in a complex organization. In the process of managing organization change it is important to be politically astute and to identify potential powerful sources of resistance.

Common sources of power include:

O organized labour;

O the power of expertise, knowledge or talent;

O the power of charismatic leadership;

O the power that comes from exercising control over key resources;

O the power that resides in the organization's traditional beliefs and values.

Any one or indeed all of these power sources can be used as the base from which resistance to organizational change is waged. It is a great mistake to believe that such powerful counterforces can be ignored and that the backing of the board of directors will be sufficient in itself to ensure a successful programme of implementing change.

Potential sources of resistance of this kind must be identified in advance and, if possible, their commitment to the proposed changes secured. Where this is not possible a power struggle will inevitably follow – a struggle that the board must win without the kind of compromise that will jeopardise the achievement of the objectives of the change programme. If necessary, powerful individuals must be removed from the positions of power in the process.

HOW THINGS CAN GO WRONG

In one major British company the organizational change programme threw up some important lessons in respect of pitfalls to avoid:

O It is a mistake to try to change everything at once – people need some stability to hold on to.

O Managers can become infatuated with the process of change *per se* and lose sight of the objectives in terms of business performance.

○ Believing that only external consultants know the answers and that one's own staff lack credibility.

○ Making experiments with new ideas usually from academic sources which have not been tried and tested in the real business environment. When these fail the whole process loses credibility.

○ 'Empowered' staff can throw out aspects of the organization's systems and procedures which previously underpinned success.

○ Management getting out of phase with the rest of the organization.

○ Change becomes synonymous with job losses and thus the very word 'change' arouses fear and anxiety.

References

1. Pascale, Richard T (1991) *Managing on the Edge,* Penguin Books, London.

2. Johnson, Gerry and Scholes, Kevan (1993) *Exploring Corporate Strategy* (3rd ed), Prentice Hall, Hemel Hempstead.

3. Burack, Elmer 'Changing the company culture – the role of Human Resource Development', *Long Range Planning* Vol 24 No 1 February 1991.

4. Beattie, Don and Tampoe, FMK 'Human Resource planning for ICL', *Long Range Planning* Vol 23 No 1 February 1990.

5. Bower, David 'Becoming a learning organization – the experience of the Rover Group' in Philip Sadler (ed) (1993) *Learning More About Learning Organizations,* AMED, London.

6. Wibberley, Martin 'Why Bosch went for Total Quality', *Personnel Management,* November 1992.

7. Harvey-Jones, John (1989) *Making It Happen,* Collins/Fontana, Glasgow.

8. Kotter, JP and Heskett, JL (1992) *Corporate Culture and Performance,* Free Press, New York.

9. Javidan, Mansour 'Leading a high-commitment, high-performance organization', *Long Range Planning* Vol 24 No 2 April 1991.

10. Cox, David L 'Doubling productivity at a major brewery', *Long Range Planning* Vol 23 No 4 August 1990.

9

Case Studies

INTRODUCTION

Each of the following cases illustrates some particular aspects of the change management process.

The Alliance & Leicester case, for example, clearly shows the importance of a strategic vision.

The BT case shows the critical importance of consistency in communication and the importance of avoiding mixed messages. The vital role of training and the need to break down traditional barriers – both functional and hierarchical – are key elements in the Fermec case.

Finally the case of The Royal Logistic Corps shows how important it is to keep a balance between tradition, which provides a reassuring link with the past, and the need for radical change.

All four cases illustrate the fact that in the context of change management there is no such thing as too much communication. They also serve to remind us of the importance of securing the commitment of middle managers and first line supervisors.

THE TRANSITION CURVE

In the BT case, Liane Parton, Employee Communications manager, talks about the transition curve. This (see Figure 9.1) is a very useful model to help understand how individuals react to change. It involves the following seven stages:

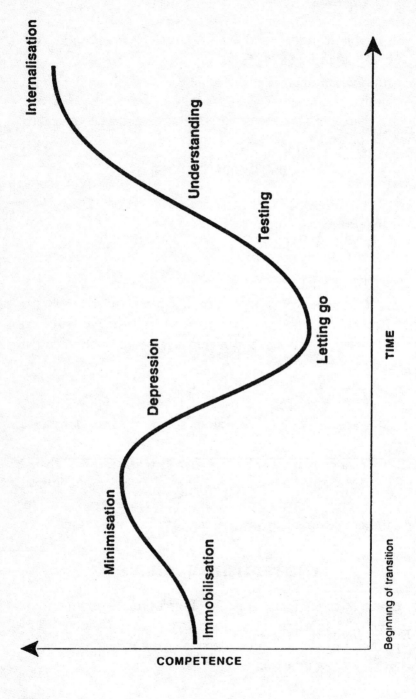

Figure 9.1 The transition curve

1. *Immobilization*. Here the feeling is that of being over-whelmed, or being unable to make plans, unable to reason and unable to understand. Many people experience this as a feeling of being frozen.

2. *Minimization*. This is a way of getting out of the first stage. Minimize the change, see it as trivial. Very often one will deny that a change even exists. This is a denial of reality which provides time for a temporary retreat from reality while an individual builds up internal strength.

3. *Depression*. As people become aware that they must make some changes in how they are living, as they become aware of the realities, they begin to get depressed. They are just beginning to face up to the fact that there has been a change. This is a time when it is difficult to know how to cope with problems, changes and life in general.

4. *Letting go*. As people become more aware of reality, they start accepting reality for what it is. Through the first three stages there is still an attachment to the past. Moving to phase four is 'unhooking' from the past (letting go). The kind of feeling may be put into words thus: 'OK, here I am now, here is what I have, here's what I want'. As this becomes accepted, feelings rise and once more optimism becomes possible.

5. *Testing*. After letting go, an individual becomes more active and starts testing the new situation, trying out new behaviours, new lifestyles, and so on. There is a great deal of energy while a person is testing new things.

6. *Understanding*. Following the burst of activity and self-testing, there is a gradual shift towards becoming concerned with understanding how things are different and why they are different. At this stage an individual tries to understand earlier behaviour, for example anger and depression.

7. *Internalization*. When an individual steps back and stops trying to understand everything, it is possible to move to the final stage of a transition. Now it is possible to incorporate

what has been learned into daily life. The change becomes a part of life. It is no longer a change. There is understanding and acceptance. This is a calm period.

THE ALLIANCE & LEICESTER

Professor Henry Mintzberg of McGill University[1] argues strongly against the conventional viewpoint that business strategy is a carefully planned process in which clear and precise objectives and the moves that are designed to achieve these objectives can be specified in advance and embodied in a corporate plan. He believes such ideas ignore the reality of organizational life and that in practice, strategy – far from being clearly thought out in advance – typically emerges from past actions. The process he describes is like the work of a potter shaping clay who is receptive to emerging – and often fortuitous – forms which are then combined with the original image to produce the finished object.

This image, of strategic change as a crafting process, is a good description of what happened at Alliance & Leicester. The 'action' which triggered the process was the opportunistic acquisition, in July, 1990, of Girobank. At the time the reasons for acquiring the bank were clear – the opportunity to acquire a current account and cheque card operation already in being, thus avoiding the expensive and protracted process of building them from scratch, plus access to Girobank's two million customers. The opportunity appeared so attractive and meeting regulatory requirements was so time consuming that all the effort was put into making the acquisition and the question of its implications for subsequent strategy was given far less attention.

Through the Girobank acquisition, Alliance & Leicester acquired some very good people and an organization with high standards of quality – it was the first financial services institution to gain BS 5750 accreditation and also to win the British Quality Award. The technical standards were high, and there was a rich store of banking expertise. Yet all this talent was being under-exploited. The business was struggling to make £25 million profit. Today it is producing over £70 million.

Rather like the person who buys a box of chattels at an auction, the Alliance & Leicester was in for some surprises once it had examined its purchase carefully. On the negative side, the active customer-base proved to be smaller and the proportion of secondary accounts higher than expected; the card operation was scarcely viable and the current account holders were mainly people accustomed to transacting their business in post offices rather than branches of banks or building societies. The most pleasing feature was the potential for Girobank's profits from cash transmission. The Bank handles a third of the country's 'high street' cash, taking it from the big retailing multiples and recycling it into post offices to pay benefits and to other 'cash consumers'. The quality of its sales force is particularly high and the activity has the great virtue of being relatively strong during periods of economic recession when other aspects of financial services go into decline.

Developing the Vision

The Society's first action following the acquisition was to establish a number of middle-level committees of managers drawn from both organizations with the aim of developing 'group policy'. In the absence of top level guidance these committees did their work without an overall vision or sense of direction and they tended to work out how to co-exist. The policies that began to emerge represented a compromise between the different viewpoints rather than a strategy designed to improve the group's performance.

Following some changes at the top of the organization, in the words of chairman Fred Crawley, 'We finally got down to doing it properly'. After taking proposals from four firms of strategy consultants, the Gemini consultancy was commissioned to help carry out a wide-ranging strategic review. New, high-level teams were set up, consisting of in-house people and Gemini consultants.

The main issue to be resolved was one of positioning. In today's highly competitive world of personal finance, building societies can be positioned on a spectrum with two extremes. At one end of the spectrum is the traditional building society, highly focused on mortgage lending and savings, with no cheque accounts, no Automatic Telling Machine (ATM) facilities and a modest retail branch network. At the other extreme is the organization with a full range of banking facilities which aims to offer across-the-board competition to the clearers. The review came to the conclusion that the first position was not viable since total reliance on the housing market was potentially dangerous. The other extreme was also ruled out on the grounds that lacking the necessary skill and experience required for a full-scale banking operation the Society would be at a competitive disadvantage against the long established clearing banks.

The decision was therefore reached to occupy a midway position, to become in effect a provider of *basic* banking services for a wide range of personal customers. Positioned at this point the business has a number of competitive advantages. It is four times as large as First Direct in telephone banking. It has preferred access to 20,000 post offices and, as a member of the Link ATM consortium, has access to 6000 units, including many at overseas locations. In addition, it has over 400 conventional building society branches and a rapidly growing field sales force.

A related strategic issue was the need to streamline the organization and to review the premises strategy. When the Alliance merged with the Leicester Building Society in 1985 the Alliance had its head office in Hove and the Leicester in Leicester itself. In order for the merger to be amicably agreed it was important that neither party should appear to emerge victorious. The decision was taken, therefore, that 49 Park Lane, London, should be the new Society's principal office – on neutral ground – and that the administrative centres in Hove and Leicester should be retained. The strategic review highlighted the burden this involved in terms of efficiency and administrative overheads and the decision was taken to close Hove and centralize all administration in Leicester, where the Society has adequate land available to accommodate its administrative activities. This move will take four years to work through and some 800 people will feel the impact of strategic change. For some, who choose to move to Leicester, it will mean a new environment, new homes, new schools for their children. For those who decide not to relocate, however, it will unfortunately mean redundancy.

The third plank of the strategy was to develop a more open management style and to develop empowerment, transferring responsibility and decision making to operating levels of the organization. In the words of the chief executive, Peter White;

> Building societies and banks traditionally have been heavily bureaucratic . . . that is the kind of climate that existed in the Alliance & Leicester . . . and to some extent still exists . . . there is no history of these conditions disappearing of their own accord. To open up an organization as big as ours demands courage. It takes commitment and real dedication.

Communicating the Vision

The process of strategic change was launched by the chairman and chief executive at a senior managers' conference in May 1993. The symbol chosen for the project was Proteus as chairman Fred Crawley explained.

> This is the title we have chosen for the strategy and its implementation. Proteus was a Greek sea-god who could change his form at will. We are going to change our form by the application of our will and our own energies; adapt, become more flexible and change to meet whatever the future demands.

The chief executive and chairman went on to outline the strategy.

> Our strategy is based on the Group – not the Society or the Bank. As a Group we have strengths on which we can build to achieve real competitive advantage – a wide variety of distribution channels, extensive product range, management skills, our image and branding and our strong business relationships.

> Our aim is to be recognized as a broad line personal financial services business, complemented by a unique corporate banking service.

> Central to the Alliance & Leicester vision is our intention to grow the value of our business and Group profits that will be the best in the industry – to be one of the most successful names in the financial services business.

We need to think, work and act as the powerful financial services group that we will become. This means a new kind of teamwork committed to the creation of a group environment where everyone is encouraged to participate – rapid development of a more open management style with contributions being valued for their contents, rather than their origins.

Change brings problems. But change isn't the enemy. It's the greatest ally of endeavour and essential ingredient of success.

Implementing the Vision

New project teams were then set up, consisting of multi-skilled personnel drawn from the Society, the Bank and Gemini. Project 'sponsors' were appointed, at executive board-level along with a steering group for the process overall, and 'champions' were appointed at general manager and assistant general manager level.

Some 35 managers below these levels were closely involved in the process at any one time, some on a semi-permanent basis, some for brief projects, as well as another 200 who were involved to a lesser degree. This helped create a widespread sense of ownership of the changes. Also the project work fostered team-building among managers from the two organizations. Ownership at board level was reinforced by frequent presentations on progress to the board as a whole, as well as one-on-one 'tutorials'.

The initial briefing for senior managers was followed by others, involving between 120 and 130 people each time. The need for constant and more effective communication was perceived early on. A special bulletin called *Proteus* was launched in June 1993 to report progress to all employees. The first issue covered the strategic vision and announced the setting up of the project groups as well as introducing the Gemini consulting group. By April 1994, 13 issues of *Proteus* had appeared. The latest issue included plans to introduce a new management appraisal system, an account of the latest senior management briefing, and brief statements on proposals to streamline the organization structure (involving the loss of about 550 jobs), and on the relocation package for those moving from Hove to Leicester. In the same issue the winners of the second batch of 'Proteus Awards' were named. This award scheme was established to recognize outstanding contributions to the change implementation programme.

At the March 1994 senior managers' briefing the chairman pointed out that implementing the strategy had turned out to be more difficult and had taken longer than was at first hoped. This had proved to be particularly true of what, he stressed, was the most important change of all – the move towards more open management and empowerment, a move involving a major culture change.

The New Values

At the same meeting the chief executive was able to announce record pre-tax profits of £205 million, up by 67 per cent on 1992. He went on to set out 'the fundamental values and beliefs' which govern 'the way we want to manage the business'. These are:

O *Honesty* – being willing to admit when we don't know the answer and reporting the bad news as well as the good.

O *Trust* – a reciprocal quality; showing trust to earn trust; learning tolerance of honest mistakes.

O *Communication* – which is about listening as much as it is about talking.

He went on to define *empowerment* and to discuss the problems involved in bringing it about.

Communication at lower levels has been achieved by a combination of the *Proteus* bulletins, the Girobank and Society newspapers (now combined into a single group publication) and team briefings, which were long established in Girobank and newly adopted by the Society.

The implementation process also involved a substantial investment in training, mainly in the form of workshops for Proteus teams and top management, each lasting between two days to a week.

Epilogue

Full integration of the Alliance & Leicester Building Society and Girobank took place on 1 May 1994, nearly four years after acquisition. The key features of integration were:

○ Girobank personal customers will be transferred to Alliance & Leicester Giro but their banking services will not be affected and their post office 'affiliation' will remain.

○ Girobank will concentrate on providing specialized banking services for corporate customers, of which by far the most important is its highly successful 'Moving Money for Business' service.

○ Plans have been completed for the launch of the 'Alliance Account', a 24-hour telephone-based current account which can also be accessed from telephones within branches. This will not involve a great deal of counter traffic and no branch level administration.

○ The Alliance Account will be the basis for a powerful cross-selling effort and for the development of a relationship-based culture on which much of the group's future progress will depend.

Meanwhile change in the competitive environment continues to accelerate and pose ever greater challenges – symbolized at this time by the Lloyds Bank bid for the Cheltenham and Gloucester Building Society.

BT

The Trigger for Change

An excellent account of the early stages of strategic change in BT is given by Höpfl, Smith and Spencer, writing in *Personnel Review*[2]. The starting point is the 1984 Telecommunications Act which not only provided for the privatization of British Telecom but also ended its status of being the exclusive provider of telecommunications services within the United Kingdom. The business now had pressures – from market analysts and institutional shareholders on one hand and from competition in the market-place on the other.

Structural Change

The initial response was structural re-organization. Twenty seven Districts were created under District General Managers and set up as semi-autonomous profit centres in an effort to move away from the previous highly centralized civil service bureaucracy. However, a review carried out a few years later in 1989 found that this structure had several shortcomings:

O The organization focused on geography rather than on customers' requirements or types of service.

O There were too many layers of management resulting in high overhead costs and slowness of response to market forces.

O There was a lack of focus for the organization as a whole as different districts followed different priorities.

A New Strategy

Following this review a new strategy was developed aimed at focusing the organization as a whole on customers' needs. This strategy, known as Project Sovereign, was launched in 1990 by Iain Vallance, BT's new chairman. Recognizing the need for a whole new approach to connecting with the customer he had introduced TQM in 1986, having seen its impact on organizations like Xerox and Motorola. A full-time project team was set up with the task of recommending 'what to do to make us customer-focused'.

The First Redundancies

This resulted in further structural change. Spans of control were widened, the layers of management were reduced to a maximum of six and 6000 management jobs were cut out. At this stage there were no redundancies below managerial level but recruitment was frozen and staff numbers began to decline through natural wastage.

The managerial redundancies were secured through a voluntary scheme known as the Management Early Release Scheme (MERS). It was targeted at managers whose jobs had disappeared under the new organization and, more generally, at those over 40 years of age. Generally, those who wished to leave were allowed to do so, and of those targeted relatively few elected to stay with the company. Many were on personal contracts which ran for 12 months and they knew that these contracts might not be renewed, leaving them jobless but without the favourable terms offered under MERS.

Under Project Sovereign the top layers of management were selected and announced first. These managers were then free to select their own teams. Once chosen, this tier was then involved in choosing the next level, and so on. This represented a major culture change from the previous situation in which vacancies were filled by promotion according to seniority as well as track record and managers had little influence on the choice of people reporting to them. Not surprisingly this process engendered a great deal of uncertainty and anxiety among the lower levels of management, many of whom were kept waiting for quite a long time before they got to know what position they would occupy.

The New Values

Morale among managers inevitably suffered in consequence. At the Chairman's Conference in November 1990 Iain Vallance acknowledged that it was 'hard going' and that BT staff were concerned that the company was abandoning its 'people values'. He re-emphasized, however, the importance of continuing to strive for Total Quality, and of working to achieve the 'vision' of the business, which was that it would become the world's top telecommunications agency. He also restated the values that characterized the new type of culture he was seeking to create:

○ We put our customers first.

○ We are professional.

○ We respect each other.

○ We work as one team.

○ We are committed to continuous improvement.

On 1 April 1990 the new organization came into effect and the radical nature of the change as a whole was symbolized by the adoption of the new logo. The structural changes and the planned changes in culture were supported by changes in processes, new performance-related payments systems and substantial bonuses for achievement against objectives. Morale began to improve.

The Role of Training

Up to this time the major changes in the organization were felt mainly at managerial levels. They were supported by extensive management training including three-day workshops on TQM and other courses such as 'Manager as Leader and Coach'. In November 1991, however, a new programme called 'Involving Everyone' was launched. This involved a thousand people a day attending one of 30 or so centres throughout the UK. At these centres, known as Event Centres, the programme started with exercises designed to communicate and reinforce the vision, the Total Quality concept and team-working. The programme was designed, however, to continue back on the job through the medium of team meetings.

The Next Wave of Redundancies – Project Release

Meanwhile, the impact of competition in the context of a severe economic recession and the activities of the Regulator made it clear that the process of organizational change was far from complete and that there was much more that needed to be done. The next step, therefore, was the Project Release.

Release 92 was without doubt the largest single 'downsizing' programme to have been carried out in the UK. Announcing it in a guide issued to all UK employees, John Steele, Group personnel director, described the scheme as offering terms for those wishing to leave the company on a voluntary basis 'significantly better than those available from other major employers in the UK'. He pointed out that BT could not guarantee to release all those who volunteered to leave.

Employees were informed about the scheme by their managers and were then given some weeks to consider whether or not to apply for redundancy. The guide referred to above enabled each person to estimate the redundancy compensation, pension and other benefits he or she would receive. It also provided information on the help and support that would be available to leavers.

Additional Benefits Packages

Employees accepted for release were invited to choose one of five additional benefit packages, as follows.

O *Training*. Open to all employees, this package was designed for those wishing to retrain in a different area of work.
   The elements comprised:

   — An interview to talk through and approve plans.

   — Advice and counselling on course selection.

   — Payment of training fees up to maxima of £4000, £3000 or £2000 according to the employee's grade.

   — Registration with a resource company (without a guarantee of work).

○ *Self employment*. Open to all employees and designed for those intending to become self-employed.

  The elements comprised:

— Professional counselling and advice, continuing in the first months after setting up in business.

— A retraining grant on a 50/50 basis with the BT contribution maximum at £500.

○ *Career change*. Open to all employees and designed for those seeking employment elsewhere.

  The elements comprised:

— A retraining grant on a 50/50 basis with a BT contribution maximum of £500.

— Outplacement service.

— A resource company to offer selected individuals a guaranteed period of temporary employment.

○ *Self help*. Open to all employees and designed for those who did not feel the other packages met their needs. Involved a cash payment of 10 per cent of pensionable pay, paid on the date of leaving.

○ *New lifestyle*. Open only to those aged 50 or over who did not intend to continue in full-time work. Included a 'new lifestyle workshop', a payment of 10 per cent of pensionable pay and, for selected individuals, registration with a resource company (without a work guarantee).

Support Services

The support services supplied by BT included:

○ *Counselling*, either with trained BT personnel or external consultants.

○ *Outplacement services*, including assistance in identifying skills and the jobs for which individuals might be best suited, advice on preparing CVs, training in interview skills and information and advice for those considering self-employment.

○ *BT 'job shops'*, providing facilities such as word processing, use of telephone, private work areas, assistance from trained staff, up-to-date lists of vacancies and copies of newspapers and journals.

○ *Retraining grants* of up to £1000 towards the cost of retraining.

○ *Employment initiatives*, which offered some opportunities for part-time and flexible working with BT and other companies.

○ *Financial advice* on such things as investments, taxation, etc.

○ *Pre-retirement seminars* for those planning to retire.

○ *A 'help desk' telephone line* staffed between 8.00am and 8.00pm Monday to Friday.

BT RELEASE 92

An Example of Redundancy Terms

Employee Aged 50

Years of reckonable service 25

Annual pensionable pay at date of leaving	£21,500
Redundancy compensation payment (6 months pensionable pay)	£10,750
Annual pension	£8,511
Lump sum	£25,533

Those employees wishing to be considered for the scheme were invited to declare their interest to their managers who would then arrange for them to receive a formal statement of benefits. Subsequently, employees wishing to proceed further would register the fact formally and BT in turn would then decide whether or not to authorize redundancy in each case. In cases where the application to leave was accepted employees were then required to reach a final decision by 17 July, for release by 31 October.

BT's target was for some 20,000 redundancies but in fact many more people – over 40,000 – wanted to take advantage of the scheme and in the end 29,000 were released under its terms. Many employees had had their hopes raised and had made plans, only to be disappointed. Management appeared to be giving mixed messages and there is no doubt that morale suffered in consequence.

BT learned some valuable lessons from this experience, particularly:

○ Don't make commitments unless you are sure they can be honoured.

○ Messages must be consistent.

○ Redundancies need to be spread out over a longer time scale.

Release 93 (Target 15,000 Voluntary Redundancies, 1993–94)

Unlike Release 92 this programme was offered on a selective basis only, to those parts of the business where reductions in staffing levels were needed. The announcement stated that BT expected to have to continue to reduce its workforce for the next few years, against a background of increasing competition, technological change, and the need to offer customers better value for their money.

The procedure adopted was as follows.

In the units chosen to participate, individuals were interviewed and the scheme explained. They were then invited to consider it and were given up to four weeks to decide whether they wished to be considered. If so, they were to register their interest with their line manager. BT would then consider the request and reach a decision within three weeks, agreeing a last day of service in the case of those accepted and providing an explanation in the case of those turned down.

This time the target was more realistic – to achieve 15,000 voluntary reductions during 1993–94. Following the lessons learned the previous year BT stressed that release under the terms of Release 93 was solely at the discretion of the company and that it was unlikely that everyone who wanted to leave would be able to.

By July 1993 7000 had volunteered and been accepted, and 8000 by August. Redeployment was also offered – from engineering and technical work to clerical jobs, allowing clerical staff to opt for release.

In September 1993 incentive payments were offered to persuade people to switch from full-time to part-time working. To qualify people had to reduce their working hours by at least 50 per cent.

By October 1993 over 10,000 had accepted a conditional offer, 4000 had expressed interest in redeployment, and 1200 in part-time working.

Since then BT has announced the introduction of a selection system for use in units expecting to have surplus staff after offering Release 93. Based on an objective points-rating system, it is applied to all managerial, professional, engineering and technical staff.

People not selected for appointment are to be designated 'supernumerary' and helped either to leave or be redeployed within BT. The selection system takes account of performance, conduct, attendance, etc as well as skill requirements.

On 1 August 1994, with staff numbers having been cut down to around 150,000 as a result of some 90,000 redundancies since 1989, Iain Vallance issued a statement indicating a need for further shrinking of the workforce to around 100,000 before the end of the decade.

Competition in the UK from Mercury and other niche operators is intensifying and regulatory pressures becoming more strict. Internationally BT faces rich and powerful competitors such as AT&T and France Telecom. Modernisation of technology increasingly means a reduced need for maintenance engineers.

The need to reduce numbers further was emphasized in an article in *The Independent*, 2 August 1994, which pointed out that using the measure *number of telephone lines per employee* BT compared unfavourably with its overseas counterparts, having 152 lines per employee at the end of 1993 compared with more than 250 for the average regional telecommunications company in the USA, 240 in Italy and 238 in Holland. A reduction in the number of employees to 100,000 would give BT a figure of 230.

FERMEC

When Richard Robson came to Trafford Park in 1987 to take over as chief executive of the Massey Ferguson plant it was, he says, 'like going back in time'. The language in use, people's attitudes and the general air of inertia were reminiscent of the 1960s and 1970s. Having previously worked for Perkins Engines and at the Varity Group's headquarters in North America he had been accustomed to more progressive policies.

A Traditional British Factory

The Trafford Park plant up to 1984 had been a satellite plant serving the main Massey Ferguson factory in Coventry and making fabrications for farming machinery. Its culture was linked to Coventry and to practices such as piecework and those established by the Coventry Toolroom Agreement. This 'feeder' role meant that any stoppage of work at Trafford Park would have stopped the main plant at Coventry. In consequence it was difficult to confront some of the issues and attitudes which needed to be changed. This constraint on management was a powerful one but nevertheless the previous factory manager, Bill Wood, had achieved considerable progress. He was appointed personnel director in 1989 following Robson's arrival and played a prominent role in the change programme from that time on.

A New Role

During 1985–86 MF Industrial was formed following a strategic decision by the parent company Varity. Fabrication of parts for Coventry ceased. A sales and marketing function was established and an engineering team set up. The new company was to design, manufacture and market 'yellow machinery', ie diggers and loaders.

The problems remaining in 1987 when Robson took over, following a loss-making year, called for more radical and more rapid change than had been achieved hitherto. A rising demand due to the boom of the late 1980s coupled with a favourable £–$

exchange rate gave the company a breathing space and a window of opportunity. It made a profit in 1987, 1988 and the first half of 1989. Robson, however, was concerned about quality, which at this time was only so-so, about the degree of overstaffing, about the lack of co-operation between functions, and about the sharp divide between management and the shop floor.

Production costs were too high, reflecting not only the over-staffing but also the lavish use of overtime and the carrying of high levels of inventory.

To help tackle these problems Robson brought in John Maguire as factory director early in 1989. Maguire was previously factory director at Oldham Batteries, part of the Hawker Siddeley Group, at Denton, Manchester. He, too, found Trafford Park something of a culture shock having come from an environment characterized by huge enthusiasm and commitment to change.

The Challenge

Together the two men began to list the things they wanted to change and which needed to change if the company were to survive. The size of the list was daunting and the scale of the task facing them was such that they feared it was impossible to achieve. One thing on the list was the need to abandon the piece-work system which was the focus of much energy-sapping conflict and had proved very expensive. The response was 'We'll shut the factory if you take the piecework system away.' They considered the possibility of such a showdown to force the issue but rejected taking a confrontational approach despite receiving a flat rejection of everything they proposed initially.

In the meantime the parent company Varity was struggling and experiencing real problems of its own. MF Industrial was competing with Perkins and Massey Ferguson for investment funding. Robson and Maguire knew they could not achieve their objectives solely through changing people's attitudes and the culture of the factory. They also desperately needed to be able to invest in new product development and in factory modernization.

The Impact of Recession

At this point the company was hit by the recession and orders fell off dramatically. The return to a loss-making situation created an atmosphere of crisis in which it became possible to act. The piecework system was finally scrapped and measured daywork substituted. At this stage, too, Robson and Maguire carefully prepared their case for new investment. The main need was for a new factory layout which would make possible a continuous flow of production from sheet steel at one end to finished vehicles at the other. To achieve this, the main capital expenditure item was a new paint plant to replace two old ones which were in the wrong places. There was also a need for additional materials-handling equipment. Robson and Maguire wrapped these items up in a total package which combined the new factory layout with the abandonment of restrictive practices and a total culture change. In short they were undertaking to transform the company's performance. The package was presented to the parent company in November 1989. Varity agreed it and undertook to make the funds available, provided that every single MF Industrial employee accepted the package too.

The 'New Deal'

In December Robson wrote to each individual employee, 800 at that time. The letter was headed MF Industrial 'New Deal'. It pointed out that the funds needed to improve the plant and equipment, and thus enable the company to survive through to the 21st century, would only be made available if all employees gave a commitment in principle to the following changes.

1. *Commitment to teamwork*
   a) Progress to 'single status' employment, eliminating differences in the treatment of employees.

b) Negotiation of and consultation relating to matters affecting all employees within the framework of a 'Company Advisory Committee' on which the three trade unions – AEU, GMB and MSF – would act as a single unit for bargaining purposes.

2. *New pay arrangements*

   a) Current hourly-paid employees to be reclassified into five grades of 'production staff'.

   b) Higher grade rates to be paid for standard performance levels with 'right first time' quality.

   c) A new bonus scheme providing for an equal bonus to be paid to all production staff.

   d) The bonus to be factory-wide, based on an index which measures British Standard hours output divided by clock hours input.

   e) A pay 'standstill' until April 1991.

   f) Current staff jobs to be reclassified as 'support staff' and a new job evaluation to be carried out on these during 1990.

   g) An understanding by the company to maintain its salary competitiveness and the merit review scheme.

By February 1990 the signatures of all 800 employees had been obtained and the road was now clear to bring about real change.

Achieving this investment had an important symbolic effect in itself, helping to change people's attitudes – particularly the cynics, including some managers who had believed they would never see the day when any significant sums of money would be spent on the plant and that ultimately closure was the only option. Attitudes were also influenced by visits from a major Japanese manufacturer of construction equipment. This company was looking for a greenfield-site joint venture agreement, which Varity declined but proposed instead that the Japanese should buy into the existing business. Following this it was possible to get project groups over to Japan to see modern working practices for themselves. People began to believe it wasn't so impossible after all.

Although negotiations for the venture eventually failed, this contact with the Japanese and the opportunity to see their methods at first-hand helped relieve a lot of the anxiety involved in moving to a 'just-in-time' continuous production system which by removing stockpiles of materials and work in progress would also remove the buffers and safety valves on which people had learned to rely in order to keep production going.

Part of the process of redesigning the production system involved the kinds of structural changes that go with the just-in-time approach: fewer levels of management and supervision; people working in multi-skilled cells; and managers having cross-functional responsibilities.

The Buy-Out

In 1992 Robson and Maguire joined with two newly recruited directors for Finance and Sales to undertake a very courageous management buy-out. Thus a new free-standing business – Fermec – was created, master of its own destiny but no longer supported by the financial strength of a major industrial group.

Robson and his colleagues were more concerned with their longer term vision of the kind of organization they were trying to build and with such issues as team-working, delegation and empowerment as the paths to sustained competitive advantage.

Throughout the period during which these changes were being made the market for 'yellow machinery' continued to decline and to meet its short-term targets the company had to make people redundant every nine months or so, mostly on a voluntary basis but ultimately some compulsory redundancy could not be avoided. In 1994 with business picking up again the company now employs some 430 people plus 30 temporary staff. A new product range has been launched and has been a considerable success, particularly in export markets. Quality is much improved. The workforce has become flexible, committed and co-operative. The time taken in 1989 to go from sheet steel to a finished product was 60 days. It is now seven or eight days.

Robson and Maguire are now able to re-focus on building for the future. Two issues concern them. First, how to maintain the momentum for change now that the crisis is over and things are on a much more even keel. Secondly, how to 'let go' and encourage further delegation and empowerment while avoiding unacceptable risks.

Training for Teamworking

In respect of both issues they have found a partial answer in training for leadership and team-working. Groups of employees – 12 at time – go to the Lake District and take part in a range of indoor and outdoor exercises. So far those attending have been at supervisory or managerial level but it is hoped to include shop-floor workers at some stage in the future. 'People who have worked here in different departments for 25 years have met each other for the first time.' The principal benefits are seen as increasing levels of mutual trust and understanding. People are learning to give and receive constructive feedback as distinct from blaming others when problems occur.

Richard Robson is quite clear in his mind that much remains to be done and that Fermec is a company in transition. Nevertheless, taking a key element in Pascale's definition of organizational transformation – that employees regard it as unrecognizable compared with what it was like before – and applying it to Fermec, it is clear that transformation is indeed an appropriate description of what has taken place.

ROYAL LOGISTIC CORPS

Today, mergers are not confined to industry and commerce. On 5 April 1993 one of the largest mergers in recent years took place when, in a single day, The Royal Logistic Corps came into being, merging the Royal Corps of Transport, the Royal Army Ordnance Corps, the Royal Pioneer Corps, the Army Catering Corps and the Postal and Courier function of the Royal Engineers.

This major change in the structure of a large section of the British Army was the outcome of a review (the Logistics Support Review) which reported in 1991, was endorsed by the Army Board in January 1992 and which recommended the change on the grounds that it would lead to improved efficiency and effectiveness.

The new organization is sizeable, comprising some 15 per cent of the Army's regular staff and 19 per cent of the total Territorial Army – a grand total of 26,960 officers and soldiers. Of these 75 per cent are concentrated in RLC units of various kinds while the rest are deployed in the field throughout the Army, for example, as drivers or chefs in other units. There are 31 regiments in the new Corps, each comprising between three and eight squadrons, as well as a further 50 or so squadrons attached to other formations, 10 major storage depots, a military port and eight training units. Personnel are spread throughout the world and good communications are vital.

The 'Big Bang'

On 5 April 1993, with characteristic military planning and precision, simultaneous changes were brought about right across the Army, wherever stationed. Some of these related to such things as staff structures, reporting relationships and procedures. Other changes were of a more symbolic, and often emotive, nature. These included changes in uniforms, badges, signs and even letter headings. In some cases, for operational reasons, local units had implemented some aspects of the changes in advance (in

Northern Ireland, for example), but nevertheless the degree of synchronization achieved was remarkable.

At the same time few were under the illusion that real and effective organizational change can be achieved in a single day. The 'Big Bang' of 5 April was of huge symbolic significance and showed that in seeking performance improvement the Army was deadly serious. The 'Sitrep' issued by the Director General of Logistic Support in March 1993, just prior to 'Big Bang', raised the following issues:

1. The need for processes which increased the Corps' ability to provide a flexible response to the unexpected. 'Organizations and doctrine must be clear but not prescriptive.'

2. The need to assess in-house capability in processes against the best in commercial practice (ie benchmarking).

    'The logistic support area has quite a lot to teach the outside world. . . But we could not claim to be at the cutting edge of technology, particularly in the information systems we employ to make the best use of our resources.'

3. In referring to the culture of the new organization, the Director General referred to ongoing work aimed at achieving 'the regimental synergy that we need' and the introduction of 'a wealth of historical, ceremonial, representational and financial matters associated with a new Corps'.

    Specific measures mentioned included the setting up of a regimental museum, the launching of a Royal Logistic Corps Journal, and the appointment of the Princess Royal as Colonel-in-Chief. This process – of building a common culture, creating a new sense of identity and belonging based on a shared set of values or ethos – is the least tangible but perhaps in the long run the most critical aspect of post-merger change management.

Ongoing Change

The changes on 5 April, however, were part of a larger ongoing process which is still being worked through. Not only were further structural changes to follow but there remained an enormous amount of work to be done to streamline procedures. It was also recognized that it would take some considerable time to build a common culture for the new Corps to replace or at least complement old traditional loyalties.

The main forces continuing to drive the need for radical change were making themselves felt in the context of a political setting in which, following the collapse of the Warsaw Pact, the whole role and function of the peacetime Army was under review, and an economic environment characterized by intense pressure to reduce government spending. Given this background the main pressures were:

○ The need to reduce staff and costs still further.

○ A particular (and inevitably sensitive) requirement to reduce the number of senior officer posts.

○ The requirement to respond to government pressure for the Army to adopt commercial practice, for example by establishing Agencies and running them on business lines.

○ Internal pressures as different parts of the Army competed for shares of a diminishing 'cake'.

For the senior officers of the Corps the sense of urgency was heightened by the need to be seen to be taking the initiative and to be proactive in making change happen rather than sitting back and waiting for the axe of the Defence Costs Studies to fall as change was imposed from without. Weighing these factors and interests together it was considered that there was an overwhelming argument in favour of pursuing radical change without delay.

The merger was left to settle down for some months before the change process was re-activated, although in the meantime very considerable effort was put into planning, consultation and briefings. The next wave of change focused on the structure of the Directorate at headquarters and on the base depots. At HQ a new, smaller management board was to be set up, consisting of the Director General and four brigadiers, each heading a policy directorate, and one civilian equivalent. There was to be a clear distinction between policy and its execution and five Agencies were to be established, each concerned with the execution of a discrete aspect of the Corps' business. Finally, all storage depots in the field were to be taken back into the control of the centre and rationalized. These changes were to be phased in between March 1994 and April 1995.

In a merger of this magnitude the immediate and urgent problems are inevitably those to do with structure. The new organization cannot begin to function effectively until roles, responsibilities and reporting lines have been decided upon and classified. Overlapping or duplicated functions have to be cut out, rationalization has to be effected and any cuts in staff have to be made. The pressing nature of such structural measures is all the greater when, as in this case, the reason for the merger was to achieve rationalization and savings. Nevertheless the process of effective change management involves other considerations to do with processes and with culture and the RLC merger involved considerations of these kinds also.

Resourcing Change

The biggest problem was not overcoming resistance to change but resourcing it. In a period when resources were being cut regardless, there was no slack in the system. Change management calls for high calibre people with imagination and enthusiasm. Where are these to be found when managing the ongoing operations is already stretching the available staff? This was the biggest challenge to be faced. It was found necessary to 'raid' other parts of the organization, taking as many senior majors and lieutenant colonels as possible. Even so, the organization was grossly overstretched. Working hours of 8.00am to midnight were not uncommon. There were indications of the stress created by this situation.

Resistance

Resistance, where it was encountered, came not from the ranks but from some at middle-level, from some retired senior officers (the 'history merchants') and from some in the largely civil-ianised 'big back end'. Inevitably, the leaders of the change programme had to confront sensitive issues and face up to vested interests in the status quo. A relatively large and hierarchical structure in the base area was undoubtedly good for career prospects yet it was equally clearly not the most efficient way to deliver service. A similar problem was raised by the need to match the number of highly capable senior managers (brigadiers), many of whom were young and recently promoted, with the number of posts of real responsibility needed by the new structure. The planning team strongly challenged the view that their job was only to 'fight their own corner'. 'Someone has to break the mould and the current climate is right for us to take a lead in doing so.'

References

1. Mintzberg, Henry (1994) *The Rise and Fall of Strategic Planning*, Prentice Hall, New York.
2. Höpfl, Heather, Smith, Sheila and Spencer, Sharon 'Values and valuations: The conflicts between culture change and job cuts', *Personnel Review* Vol 21 No 1 1992.

Further Recommended Reading

Burnes, Bernard (1992) *Managing Change*, Pitman, London.

Coulson Thomas, Colin (1992) *Transforming the Company*, Kogan Page, London.

Hastings, Colin (1993) *The New Organization*, McGraw-Hill, Maidenhead.

Hendry, J, Johnson, G and Newton, J (eds) (1993) *Strategic Thinking. Leadership and the Management of Change*, John Wiley, Chichester.

Moss Kanter, R, Stein, BA and Jick, TD (1992) *The Challenge of Organizational Change*, Free Press, New York.

Pettigrew, Andrew and Whipp, Richard (1993) *Managing Change for Competitive Success*, Blackwell Business, Oxford.

Sadler, Philip (1994) *Designing Organizations* (2nd edn), Kogan Page, London.

Tichy, NM and Devanna, MA (1986) *The Transformational Leader*, John Wiley, New York.

Wille, Edgar and Hodgson, Philip (1991) *Making Change Work*, Mercury/Gold Arrow, London.

Wilson, DC (1993) *A Strategy of Change*, Blackwell, Oxford.

Index